Update

Update is a unique project in educational publishing. It is aimed at A-level students and first-year undergraduates in geography. The objective of thc series, which ranges across both physical and human geography, is to combine the study of major issues in the geography syllabus with accounts of especially significant case studies. Each *Update* incorporates a large amount of empirical material presented in easy-to-read tables, maps and diagrams.

Update is produced from the Department of Geography at Queen Mary and Westfield College (QMW) by an editorial board with expertise from across the fields of Geography and Education. The editor is Roger Lee.

We hope that you find the series as exciting to use as we find it to produce. The editor would be delighted to receive any suggestions for further *Updates* or comments on how we could make the series even more useful and exciting.

Preface

Care of, and concern for, the environment in which we live is not a new phenomenon; for example, the seeds of the National Park movement date back to the 1870s. However, the past 25 years have witnessed an unprecedented surge of interest in, and debate about, the environment. The same period has seen some of the most damaging changes to the environment.

For many years environmental issues were essentially of local, or, rarely, regional extent. One major exception was the debate over radioactive fallout which culminated in the international agreement to abolish the testing of atomic weapons in the atmosphere, drawn up in the 1950s. Today local and regional issues are still important, but global warming, tropical forest destruction and desertification have become more prominent.

Hand in hand with the incrcasing scale of the issues has come the awareness that in most instances the nature of the problem is more complex than initially envisaged, and that solutions to the problem are more difficult.

Ever since the pioneering space-flights of the 1960s the idea of the planet Earth as a single functioning unit has gained ground. There has been talk of the 'global village'; there have been influential studies such as 'Global 2000'; there have been notable meetings such as the 'Earth Summit' of 1992. All these, and others, have increased awareness of environmental issues and increased research into the nature of the problems.

That parts of the environment are seriously threatened by human activities has gained credence over the past 25 years as observation and monitoring have increased our understanding of how the planetary systems function. The extent of the problem, however, remains debatable. At one extreme lies the doomsday scenario that the planet as we know it is on the brink of destruction. At the other extreme, many equally well informed people point to the immense self-regulating capacity of the planet, and argue that none of the acknowledged problems are insurmountable.

What is clear, however, is that, first, the capacity now exists to monitor environmental change at a scale and at a level of detail that was impossible only a decade ago. Second, the astonishing complexity of the inter-relationships between the several parts of the natural environment are being revealed. Third, human activity has profoundly influenced the natural environment, and as technology has developed, this influence has increased in both scale and complexity. Fourth, our developing technology does enable humans to reverse some established trends and modify others. Fifth, technical solutions can only be implemented if the correct socio-economic conditions are in place. Finally, while human activities continue to degrade the environment there is a clear link between environmental disruption and global population numbers.

Contents

Introduction

Fundamental inter-relationships exist between the climate, vegetation, soils and landforms of Earth. As the genus *Homo* evolved, its intervention in this natural order gradually increased. At first it was merely an additional factor, even when fully evolved into *Homo sapiens*. However, at some point in the past human numbers and skills began to leave a recognizable imprint upon this natural order. The date varies from place to place. Radiocarbon dating of human occupation sites in northern Australia indicate that interference was in progress 35,000 BP; in Papua New Guinea a figure of 9,000 BP has been determined. In Britain the first clear signs of activity date from the Mesolithic period. There are no compelling reasons for thinking these are the earliest dates.

While human numbers remained small and the technology limited, interference was patchy, rarely of long duration, and largely restricted to modifications of the vegetation. That position has changed dramatically over the past few hundred years as world population numbers have increased, and technologies developed, to the point where human beings are now an extremely potent factor. They have not only greatly altered the patterns of natural vegetation, they have modified soil conditions over large areas, changed the composition of the atmosphere and modified the contours of the land surface.

Until recently much of this was achieved on the unstated premise that *Homo sapiens* had risen above nature. A growing body of opinion now accepts, however, that not only are localized environmental accidents often an unnecessary 'own goal', but that this dominance over the natural order has been achieved through exploitation and destruction without the understanding necessary for the continued safe functioning of the planet. In other words, our human species has to live within certain constraints. Of these constraints the condition of the atmosphere is the most fundamental, for in spite of showing greater adaptability to different climates than almost any other species of animal or plant, the fact remains that human organization across the world is based largely upon the continuance of the existing patterns of air temperature and precipitation, and more importantly upon the existing forms and strengths of solar radiation.

Today there are worrying signs that by our polluting the atmosphere in various ways changes are taking place in the nature of the ozone layer, which acts as an important filter for solar radiation, and in the gaseous composition of the atmosphere, and that these changes are leading to the 'greenhouse' effect. The occurrence of damaging acid rain, radioactive contamination, localized air pollution, soil erosion and species extinction are but a few of the many instances resulting from the mismanagement of the environment.

In recent years environmental issues have become matters of concern for a growing number of people and there are now many examples of attempts to curb the worst excesses of human action, and to rehabilitate damaged ecosystems. Much of this work has been funded by the United Nations, by aid agencies such as Oxfam, and by conservation groups such as the World Wide Fund for Nature. There are, too, national and local, professional and amateur bodies working towards these ends.

Many of the examples of mismanagement of the natural environment affect only a limited area but some have a much wider impact. These transnational, even global, problems have only begun to emerge over the past two decades, unlike the local problems, many examples of which can be identified from historic records. Explaining the global problems and devising remedies is a scientific and technical challenge. Implementing these remedies is largely a political decision.

This *Update* provides a framework within which some of the more topical issues of environmental concern are considered. The approach is largely through the use of case studies. These are drawn from various parts of the world as appropriate but tend to focus on British, European and South-West Pacific examples, areas with which the author is particularly familiar.

1 The atmosphere: benevolent dustbin

Introduction

The composition and characteristics of the atmosphere are fundamental to the functioning of almost all lifeforms and influence most surface relief features of planet Earth, as well as determining the distribution of the major soil groups. Spatial variations in the atmosphere, particularly with respect to temperature and moisture content, are of prime importance in determining the major ecological divisions of Earth.

The atmosphere is the air we breathe. Close to the surface, up to 15 km, it is the fluid turbulent gaseous envelope that is our weather and climate. At higher levels, although increasingly rarified and less turbulent, it acts as a vital buffer to the incoming solar radiation emitted by the Sun, absorbing X-rays, short ultraviolet rays and ultraviolet rays. It thus acts as a second line of defence, behind the magnetosheath, against the deadly radiation of the protons and electrons of the solar wind that stream out from the Sun through space at approximately one and a half million kilometres per hour (fig. 1).

The importance of the total atmospheric envelope (fig. 2) is underlined by the discovery in the past ten years of holes in the ozone layer within the stratosphere that permit the entry of harmful ultraviolet rays. These holes are possibly the result of industrial pollution from chlorofluorocarbons (CFCs) or jet aircraft and close monitoring reveals that they are tending to grow year by year.

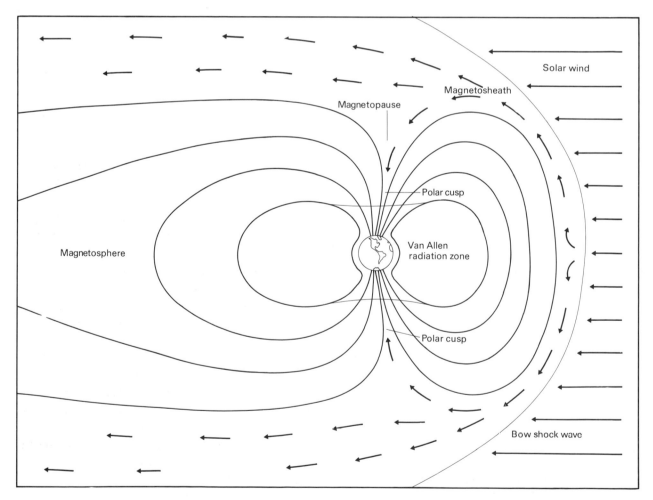

Figure 1　　**A magnetic envelope, the magnetosheath, shelters Earth from the full effects of the solar wind. The atmosphere is our second line of defence.**
Source: Allen (1983)

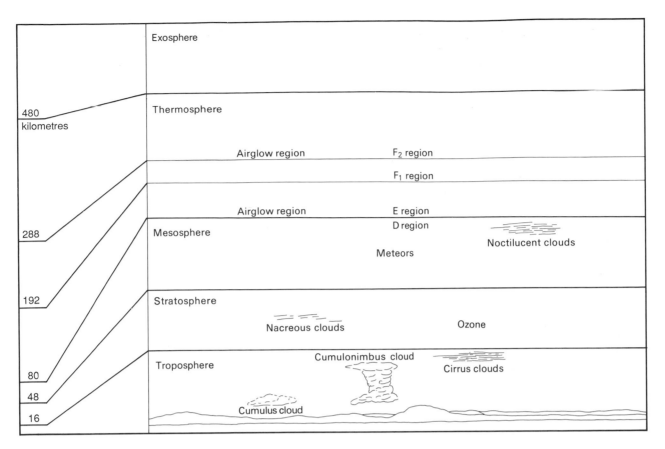

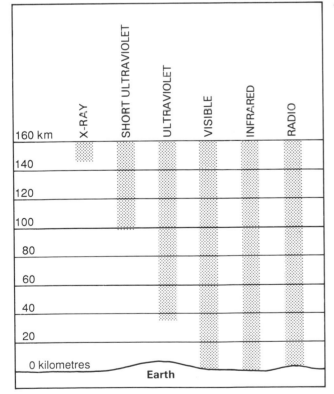

Figure 2 **Schematic diagram of the atmospheric layers, with (top) actual dimensions and (above) the filtering effect of the atmosphere upon X-rays and ultraviolet rays.**
Source: Allen (1983)

The value of atmosphere

The atmosphere is a resource of the whole world. It is also a national resource insofar as it is one of the factors limiting economic activity in any one country. At a smaller scale it may be a resource utilized by individuals, be they farmers, fishermen, ice-cream sellers or industrialists. Viewed as a resource, the atmosphere becomes something to be used efficiently rather than something to be regarded merely as an ever-present, largely benign component of the environment. It is, however, a variable resource in both the spatial and temporal senses. Atmospheric conditions in Iceland are not the same as those in Italy, for example. Seasonal changes in temperature and precipitation occur over a time scale of months during which there may also be shorter variations in temperature, rainfall or windspeeds.

As a resource it is necessary to understand how the atmosphere works and especially how it is going to change in future. For many purposes advanced warning of change of a few hours, a day, a week, a month, or even a year is valuable. The understocked ice-cream seller can only lament a past heatwave. Stocks could be laid in for the heatwave to come. Likewise the electric power generating industry needs to know of forthcoming cold spells, or with air-conditioning, heatwaves.

Reaction times to changes vary according to the use being made of the resource. The power generating industry can respond very quickly so that forecasts for the next 12 hours will be valuable; so too can an airline pilot. A farmer, on the other hand, may need weeks, if not months, of advance warning in order to complete or modify farming activities. In these circumstances the need for long-range forecasts becomes clear.

So far it has been assumed that the variations occur within an unchanging climate. In such circumstances a severe drought or flood, or even two or three in rapid succession, are seen merely as blips within the long period of quasi-constant climate. However, there is an overwhelming amount of evidence, not least that pointing to the vastly more extensive sheets of ice during the relatively recent past, which indicates that long-term climatic changes have taken place and continue to occur. Measuring and understanding these present-day climatic changes is of fundamental importance, because adjusting to the consequences initiated by such changes may take decades. For example, it may prove necessary to breed new strains of our existing crops or it may be necessary to relocate millions of people living in low-lying coastal areas.

Acceptance of the atmosphere as a resource not only requires that it should be used efficiently (and that the data are available to enable this to occur) but also that it should not be despoiled. Diverting a hurricane onto a less damaging track by cloud seeding (a science fiction concept as yet) may be acceptable; polluting the atmosphere with gaseous or particulate material may not be. Atmospheric pollution is now regarded by many people across the world as a major environmental problem with potentially catastrophic consequences if unchecked.

As indicated above, the atmospheric conditions occurring at a particular place are rarely constant. Nevertheless there is usually a daily or annual pattern (almost never identical) to temperature, precipitation and wind conditions which when averaged over a period of years produces what most people recognize as the climate of the area. The social, and part of the economic, structure of an area are usually adjusted to these average conditions. The timing of Henley Regatta, Wimbledon and the Lord's Test reflects in part an underlying climatic influence. Likewise lifestyles in suburban Canberra, Australia, differ from those

in suburban Oslo, Norway, without necessarily being better or worse.

Short-term oscillations about the average which take the form of storms, heatwaves, cold snaps, droughts, etc. form one group of atmospheric phenomena, each of which imposes a cost upon the people of the area affected and probably gives a financial benefit to a few. No less important are the variations in the seasonal weather conditions. In this category one might place cooler-than-average springs, damp summers, or dry autumns, since at least as far as agriculture is concerned quite small deviations from the norm can have a big impact upon the eventual yields.

The above changes may be merely deviations about nearly constant average conditions. However, from a longer-term perspective the average conditions may also be changing. This knowledge may be of considerable importance to the farmers of an area and to a country as a whole, but so too is the nature of the change. Is it, for example, part of a long-term trend to generally warmer (cooler) or drier (wetter) conditions or is it merely part of a cyclical event? If the latter, what is the length of the cycle? Is it seven years, eleven years, nineteen years or perhaps one to be measured in decades? Clearly knowledge of future trends could have important geopolitical as well as economic consequences.

In a single day probably more high-quality data are handled and processed by the Meteorological Office at Bracknell, Berkshire, than are available to the British Treasury in a year. Even so, while 24-hour weather forecasts have a generally good record of accuracy in spite of public perceptions to the contrary and in spite of some acknowledged errors, long-term forecasts (those for more than two weeks ahead) are still in their infancy. In contrast, economic data, even in Britain, are still very unreliable and are rarely up to date. Many are at least a month old before being published; some are even more out of date. In addition economic information is usually consolidated into industrial groups or into specific regions so obtaining data for a precise location is very difficult.

This mismatch of meteorological and economic data makes it very difficult to calculate the value of climate and weather to the national economy as a whole or to a specific region. However, the obvious economic gains to be derived from establishing links between the two data sets have encouraged much work to be done (Mason, 1966; Maunder, 1970; 1971; 1986; 1989). At first this work could only be applied to past conditions (Maunder, 1966) and especially to agricultural production. In this sphere, as the links between climate and output have been unravelled and as computing power has increased, it has become possible to use climatic parameters, updated to the present, to predict yields up to several months in the future. Already in New Zealand the marketing of some agricultural products is influenced by the projected output. The potential importance of this approach increases as longer-range forecasts become available.

Many other industries are climate- and weather-sensitive. Some, such as the electric power generating industry in Britain, already make full use of the available data; others do not. As long-range forecasts become more reliable many more firms will recognize their economic value and join the long list of those who already base decisions on the existing short-range forecasts.

Some indication of the mismatch of data might highlight this point. The first example concerns the tragic fire at York Minster in 1985. If it is accepted that the fire was caused by lightning, then the repair costs can reasonably be attributed to an explicable weather event. Four years later there was still no precise figure of the repair costs. The 'many millions of pounds' postulated in the national press immediately after the event is still the best estimate.

A second British example illustrates the problem even better. In October 1987 a severe storm swept across southern Britain. Although it took the weather forecasters by surprise subsequent analysis has meant that the meteorological conditions are now known in immense detail. Indeed, much was known less than twenty-four hours after the event. This material is now readily available in the scientific literature (Burt and Mansfield, 1988; Morris, 1988; Reynolds, 1988). In contrast, the economic costs of the storm are still a mystery. For example, the precise number and details of insurance claims of all the individuals to the many insurance companies is a matter for conjecture. Technically it must be possible to accumulate this information but the research effort needed would be immense. Other costs, too, remain unknown. What did it cost the Central Electricity Generating Board (CEGB) to repair its transmission lines? How much did the storm cost British Rail for

clearing blocked lines, and loss of revenue through cancelled services? What did it cost local councils, and industry and commerce, through late arrivals of workers or absenteeism as individuals battled to clear up the mess? A best guess of hundreds of millions of pounds is probably as near as one can get, and this was a figure published in the newspapers before the full extent of the damage was known. The contrast with the meteorological data is striking.

It is a similar story with Hurricane Gilbert, which struck the Caribbean in September 1988 (fig. 3). The meteorological conditions associated with this tropical storm were monitored with care and great accuracy. Interpretations of synoptic data were based on information obtained only minutes earlier, and forwarded to key civil defence personnel almost as quickly. Subsequently the synoptic data have been re-analysed and the findings published (Eden, 1988). The human and economic consequences are, in contrast, more difficult to pin down. Data on structural damage to buildings and the effects on the economies of the affected countries, even on deaths, were and remain imprecise and fragmented. Reports at the time suggested one-fifth of the housing stock of Jamaica was wiped out and 500, 000 (one-fifth of

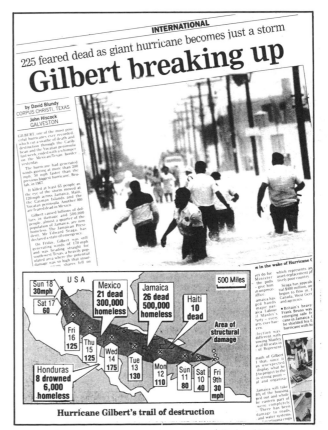

Figure 3 Newspaper report on Hurricane Gilbert.
Source: *Sunday Telegraph*, 18 September 1988

Table 1 Estimated 'costs' of the 1969/70 drought in New Zealand

Item	Reason	Assuming high cost $NZ	Assuming low cost $NZ
Livestock	Stock movement	500,000	250,000
Wheat	Lower production	5,000,000	3,000,000
Fertilizer	Subsidies	6,750,000	2,700,000
Drought relief	Budget provision	3,800,000	2,850,000
Rural lending	Budget provision	6,000,000	2,000,000
Dairy production	Lower production	15,000,000	6,800,000
Lamb production	Lower production	1,500,000	1,000,000
Wool production	Lower production	4,480,000	2,700,000
Total		$43,030,000	$21,300,000

Source: Maunder (1971)

the population) were made homeless. No verification or refinement of these figures has appeared subsequently and it must remain doubtful if an accurate final count was ever made. Damage to Jamaica was put at $8 billion by the (then) Prime Minister Edward Seaga. Even at half this total it represents an incredible asset replacement task for a relatively poor country. The point being made here, however, is that the figure was little more than (another) best guess, possibly politically inspired in view of the nearness of national elections. A year later this figure was as enigmatic as ever. The contrast with the meteorological data is again striking, and was repeated when Hurricane Hugo struck the Caribbean in 1989.

Variations in the yield of field crops and the output from animals can be demonstrated to be linked to climatic conditions, not least because agricultural statistics are one of the more accurate items of annual economic data. Assessing the impact of climate upon a growing crop is much less accurate, as can be seen by comparing the astonishingly high price of coffee futures when a late frost is reported in Brazil with the much lower price (usually) when harvesting has taken place.

Crop yield may be affected by a range of climatic conditions. In both 1987 and 1988 yields in the United Kingdom of crops such as wheat, barley and rape were well below the average for the previous five years. Since neither 1987 nor 1988 were astonishingly bad climatically, the precise

cause of the disappointing yields is difficult to pinpoint. In some areas the relatively mild winter of 1987/88 encouraged fungal diseases among standing crops. Too much rain in the spring of 1987 and in July and August 1988, coupled with the associated lack of sunshine and warmth, was perhaps the major factor. Not enough of the right conditions at the right time probably sums up the situation most aptly. The net result was that the cereal harvest in 1988 of just in excess of 21.3 million tonnes (it was almost the same in 1987) was more than 5 million tonnes less than in the bumper year of 1984. In the arcane world of agricultural prices it is not possible to calculate the exact loss of income this represents to farmers generally, still less what it meant for individual farmers. Nevertheless one can state that, because of the climatic conditions in 1988, less cereals were produced than expected and therefore some farmers at least received less money, even if it is uncertain what use any greater output might have been put to and who might have paid for it. The yield for 1989 was similarly disappointing due to the unusually dry conditions with a total of 22.4 million tonnes produced.

Few advanced nations of the world are as dependent upon agriculture, and especially livestock agriculture, as New Zealand. Of New Zealand's total gross domestic product in 1984/85 11.4% was from the agricultural production sector and 6.1% from the food production sector. At the same time almost 70% of exports were agriculturally based.

Table 2 Performance of United Kingdom industries in relation to short-term climatic variations

Industry	Average deviation per month from mean of preceding season	
	1962/63 winter	1976 summer
Bricks, cement etc.	− 14.4	− 0.9
Timber, furniture	− 14.3	− 1.8
Clothing and footwear	− 9.6	+ 3.0
Paper, printing and publishing	− 5.6	− 2.2
Mining and quarrying	− 4.7	− 2.3
Shipbuilding	− 4.3	− 0.9
Drinks and tobacco	− 2.4	+ 4.4
Ferrous metals	− 2.3	− 10.0
Chemicals	− 0.6	+ 2.1
Textiles	0.0	− 0.6
Utilities	+ 17.5	− 6.4

Sources: Maunder and Ausubel (1985); Palutikof (1983)

The links between climatic conditions in New Zealand and farm output have been studied in detail by Maunder (1966; 1970; 1986) and by the NZ Meteorological Service. Two examples will be given here. The first details the estimated costs of the 1969/70 drought (Maunder 1971; 1986). These are expressed in table 1.

If these figures are broadly correct (and they necessarily involve many assumptions) it means that the cost of this drought to the New Zealand economy as a whole exceeded 3% of the total value of exports in that year.

Nor are droughts particularly uncommon in New Zealand. Other examples include the 1981/82 drought in Canterbury and the 1988/89 drought, which also affected the South Island in particular. In both cases all farming activities were adversely affected. Estimates suggest that the 1988/89 drought reduced the lamb crop by 1.7 million animals (3.6%) compared to the previous year. This was reflected in lower export numbers. In addition the lambs took longer to reach the required export weight. All of this represents either a loss of income or an additional cost to the farmer and the country.

It must not be thought, however, that climatic variations are the only influence on agricultural output. General economic conditions nationally and internationally, cultural factors and political influences, all play their part. Although the mild, maritime, equable climate has been seen as the cornerstone underpinning the industry in New Zealand, its success has been partly explained in terms of technology, innovations, breeding techniques, animal and pasture care, financial incentives, marketing and the land-holding system which has encouraged owner occupiers. However, output also reflects the investment put into farming. This is expressed in a Reserve Bank of New Zealand publication (Walsh, 1981) which lists in order of importance (a) monetary terms of trade, (b) climatic conditions and biological factors, (c) technical change and innovation and (d) the availability of resources of land, labour and credit. Since investment takes several years to work through a system it can be seen that poor climatic conditions, particularly in successive years, reduce farmers' confidence and farm income for reinvestment. This may result in lower productivity several years later as well.

As hinted at earlier it is not only the agricultural sector that is influenced by changes in the atmospheric conditions. Damage caused by severe meteorological events such as storms has already been mentioned. However, changes in economic activity can also be brought about by less violent conditions. A survey conducted in 1983 by British Rail into why more trains run late in wet weather is one interesting example. The study by Palutikof (1983) into the impact of the severe 1962/63 winter and the severe drought of 1976 in Britain is another example (table 2).

This analysis showed that certain sectors of the economy recorded distinct changes when compared with the preceding season, most notably the 17.5% increase in utilities in the 1962/63 winter and the jump in drinks and tobacco output in the hot summer of 1976.

Although one of the limits put upon agriculture is the climate of an area, when viewed as a resource it can be said that farmers use the existing climate to their best advantage. The same applies to a lesser extent to many industries. However, in at least one context – wind power – the atmosphere is used directly. Historically this source of energy has been harnessed by sailing ships and windmills. Renewed interest in wind power has been shown recently in the quest for alternative sources of energy. Wind-generated turbines have been one outcome and are in use in several areas, notably Altamont Pass, California, and in Jutland, Denmark. In Britain a prototype design has been established on Burgar Hill in the Orkney Islands. A second modern use has been to augment ships' engines by means of computer-controlled rigged plastic sails. Few vessels have yet adopted this technology although the Japanese registered oil tanker *Shin Aitoku Maru* is a working example. If applied to all new vessels the eventual saving on fuel consumption, even if only 10%, would be substantial.

Utilizing the power of the Sun's rays is another direct use of the atmosphere. In recent years the installation of solar panels in buildings to heat water has become quite common in countries with a high sunshine record such as Israel, Australia and in California, USA. Concentrating the Sun's rays by means of mirrors to create enough heat to produce steam to drive turbines to generate electricity is another modern development. The solar energy generator at Font Romeu high in the eastern Pyrenees, France, is one interesting example of this use of the atmosphere.

This section has shown that not only does the atmosphere have a profound influence on human activities but that it is also being utilized as a resource. Considerable research effort has been directed at modifying some aspects of the atmosphere and harnessing other aspects. However, by far the greatest gains have been made in our understanding of the atmosphere and from this being able to forecast conditions to come. Further developments in this area can be expected in view of the economic importance attached to this information.

Modifying the atmosphere

Viewing the atmosphere as a resource, it is advantageous to utilize it as fully as possible. In agricultural terms one can do this by (a) forecasting future patterns and so optimizing beneficial periods and minimizing adverse conditions, (b) using or breeding plant strains that are better suited to local conditions, or (c) modifying the atmosphere condition to some extent. Available moisture, temperature and windspeed have all been modified in an effort to increase productivity or take advantage of market conditions.

Increasing the available water is most easily done by irrigation, which in one sense is transferring the benefits of high rainfall in one area to another area. Irrigation along the Nile in Eygpt is really utilizing the surplus rainwater of Ethiopia, for example. Irrigation using wells is, in effect, often utilizing surplus rainfall from past climatic conditions.

The technique of irrigation dates back into ancient history. In Iran, for example, there is a network of many thousands of kilometres of aqueducts that was begun by the Persians in the 7th century BC. In North Africa, the Middle East, India and Pakistan, to name only a few areas, irrigation is a major factor in agricultural production. In the past 50 years there has been a major expansion of the technique following improved and cheaper technologies and the development of schemes designed to avoid such problems as salt accumulation in the soil. In the western states of the USA the amount of irrigated land more than doubled between 1940 and 1980.

A more direct method of modifying the atmosphere to increase precipitation is to seed clouds with dry ice or silver iodine in an effort to create raindrops. Considerable research effort was directed at this problem in the 1940s and 1950s, notably in the USA (Havens *et al.*, 1978). In scientific terms the tests were not entirely a failure, but producing rain precisely when and where it was needed and in exactly the right quantity could not be achieved. Irrigation was infinitely preferable.

Cloud seeding has also been used in an attempt to reduce the intensity of hurricane windspeeds on the theory that by accelerating the transformation of liquid water to ice the latent heat of fusion would be released, thereby increasing the temperature at the release point. At first this was directed at the eye-wall in order to reduce the temperature differential and relieve the pressure forces that kept it in a tight spiral. With a larger diameter wall the windspeeds should be reduced. After inconclusive results following the seeding of Hurricane Betsy in 1965 attention then shifted to seeding areas outside the eye-wall in an attempt to create new centres of turbulence and hence spread the available energy more widely but more thinly. Hurricane Debbie (1969) was targeted and windspeeds were diminished by 16% and their potential destructiveness by up to 50%. However, hurricane tracks are subject to sudden changes in direction and while the damage from an unseeded storm may be great at least it is regarded as a natural disaster. If a storm is seeded it can be argued that this also interfcres with the storm track and therefore any damage is partly the result of the intervention, since had it been left alone the storm might have taken a different path. Faced with these and other difficulties the manipulative research effort has been scaled down and funds directed more at improving hazard warning systems (Pielka, 1990).

Attempts at modifying temperature and windspeed are, in comparison, much more primitive and usually involve the erection of some form of barrier. One of the earliest techniques was to build a walled garden, which has the advantage of both providing shelter from the winds and raising temperatures by reradiating the heat from the bricks. A second technique is to use greenhouses or cloches to create an artificial microclimate. The advent of plastic has greatly expanded this method.

A third technique is to grow shelter belts, mainly to reduce windspeed, to lessen damage to the crops, or to inhibit soil erosion. Many of the orchard and market garden areas in the south of France exposed to the mistral or tramontane winds are protected in this way. So too are citrus fruit, tamarillo and kiwifruit orchards in the Kerikeri area of North Auckland, New Zealand. On a more extensive scale shelter belts (often of exotic trees such as *Macrocarpa* sp. and *Eucalyptus* sp.) form a feature of the landscape of the Canterbury Plains, New Zealand, where field trials have recently shown that yields may be increased by up to 35% when given protection (Sturroch, 1981; Holland, 1988).

While specific attempts have been made to improve the climatic conditions for crop growth it should also be noted that by clearing the land of its natural vegetation cover and replacing it with crops, farmers have greatly modified the micro-climate. The amount of rainfall reaching the ground, windspeed patterns and temperature patterns at the micro-level are all modified to some extent.

Much the same occurs in urban areas, where a distinct urban climate can be recognized in the larger cities. The heat-island caused by the absorption and reradiation by buildings and roads of the Sun's rays is a particularly well known effect (Chandler, 1965; Oke, 1988). Just as noticeable are changes to the windspeed and wind direction particularly in towns with high-rise blocks. Building design can play a significant role in increasing or reducing this factor and making areas attractive or unattractive for pedestrians.

Atmospheric changes consequent upon the building of towns and cities do occur but few, if any, attempts have been made to actually alter the external climate. Instead, attempts are made to isolate the individual from the external climate by the specific design of a building, by technological means such as heating and cooling systems, or by providing large covered spaces.

Atmospheric pollution

In its natural state the atmosphere is not unpolluted. Windblown dust particles are carried into it from desert regions, volcanoes belch forth both particles and gases as do lightning fires in grasslands and forests. Cosmic dust filters down from the stratosphere. However, the scale of the natural pollutants in relation to the total atmosphere is under present conditions minute. Nor, until recently, were the polluting effects of human beings much greater. It is true that one can cite early examples of local pollution – the corrosion of the stones of St Paul's Cathedral in London, burnt down in the Great Fire of 1666, was caused by acid rain derived from the city's chimneys – but widespread damage had to await industrialization and the explosion of human population over the past 200 years (Sharp *et al.*, 1982). Even so, the actual amount of particles and gases created by humans is small compared with that from natural sources. It is the nature and style of pollution that is so important.

Atmospheric pollution takes two basic forms: it may be particulate or gaseous. Its consequences are more varied. It may result in illness or death among human beings; it may reduce visibility and endanger transport sytems; it may interact with the atmosphere and cause increases in precipitation or higher temperatures. Its effects may be direct or indirect, simple or complex, self-regulating or possibly self-sustaining (Elsom, 1987).

Particulate pollution

Compared with the 1200 million tonnes of particles of natural origin that enter the atmosphere each year, the 92 million tonnes created by human activities may seem quite modest. However, these latter particles are often smaller and so remain airborne longer, are concentrated into specific areas, and generally are of a type more dangerous to health. The inefficient burning of coal accounts for more than one-third of the total.

Problems with particle-laden smoke date back several hundred years and the relationship between this type of air pollution and respiratory illnesses was well understood. Nevertheless it was not until the 1930s that the dangers reached severe proportions. Nor is it entirely clear why this should be so since there is scant evidence to suggest that there was more smoke and stronger temperature inversions after 1930 than before it. Perhaps the exhaust fumes from the, by then, increasing numbers of cars and buses just tipped the balance.

Undoubtedly the worst case of air pollution of this type occurred in London in December 1952. Under anticyclonic conditions an inversion of temperature developed which prevented the upward escape of cooler air from below. This air quickly became polluted from the coal fires and power stations. Visibility dropped steadily – reportedly one could not see one's feet in some areas – and smuts of soot settled on any bare surface. As time passed more and more people complained of breathing difficulties and the final death toll was approximately 4000 more than normal for that time of year. Eventually a low-pressure centre began to stir the air and disperse the smog. Faced with such a tragedy Parliament quickly brought in laws to reduce smoke emissions and within a decade London had been transformed into a relatively smog-free area.

Chemical pollution

The simple act of reducing the amount of pollutants from coal fires did not work for long. In both Los Angeles and Tokyo visibility had begun to decline after about 1940 and yet coal smoke was evidently not the cause. In the early 1950s the problem became chronic. Redoubled research efforts revealed the answer. In this case exhaust emissions from the motor car proved to be the source of the trouble as they embarked on a complex chemical transformation, driven by the ultraviolet light from the Sun, from nitric oxide to nitrogen dioxide. Once again inversion conditions are necessary before a build-up of pollutants can take place. Once again strict laws, this time on exhaust emissions using a catalytic converter, did much to contain the problem.

However, exhaust fumes contain several other damaging pollutants, the control of which has become possible only as technological skills have improved. Carbon monoxide is one, exhaust lead is a second. When leaded petrol is burned millions of minute lead particles are sent into the air. The majority fall close to the roadsides as both monitoring equipment and samples of vegetation at increasing distances from the road have shown, but some remain aloft and travel great distances on the global winds as detectable lead pollution in the snow at both the North and South Poles indicates. Excessive lead levels in human beings (and presumably other organisms) can be a health hazard. However, the introduction of lead-free petrol should, like the earlier Clean Air Acts, go a long way towards controlling the problem. Carbon emissions are an important contributor to the 'greenhouse' effect. They, too, can be reduced per vehicle using new technology. The problem here is that the increasing number of vehicles threatens to outweigh the savings made on each individual vehicle.

In the 1980s a new atmospheric pollutant has emerged – chlorofluorocarbon (CFC). Used as a propellant in aerosol cans and as a coolant in refrigerators and air conditioners, CFCs have been linked in a complex chemical chain which ultimately leads to a depletion in the upper-atmosphere ozone layer. For several years now, small but significant seasonal reductions in the amount of ozone present have been noted in the southern hemisphere over Antarctica and more recently the South Island of New Zealand. The consequence of this reduction is that more ultraviolet light reaches the surface of the planet, thereby increasing the danger of skin cancer. Further reductions would be correspondingly more serious.

In almost all these cases worthwhile reductions in the amount of pollutants entering the atmosphere can be made. They do, however, involve a cost and across the world the ability to pay that cost varies. Rich, developed nations, which have generally contributed so much to the pollution so far, can afford the newer, more expensive technology. However, the majority of the world's people are poor. They are beginning to want electric power, refrigerators, motor cars and so on. Is it fair that they should have to pay the higher prices just to ensure they don't pollute our air?

Gaining global acceptance for anti-pollution measures is close to a political nightmare. If only a few countries cause the pollution, however, effective action may be possible. This has already occurred in the case of radioactive pollution caused by the atmospheric testing of nuclear weapons. Even so, in spite of the known dangers of radioactivity to human beings, agreement between the USSR, USA and UK was only reached in 1963 after protracted negotiations. France reluctantly joined the agreement some years and several tests later, to be joined by China later still. The amount of nuclear fallout has declined dramatically since underground testing became the norm, but as the Three Mile Island and Chernobyl accidents show, pollution from civil sources can occur and there is still the long-held belief that even under the most stringent safety conditions sufficient contamination can occur to greatly increase the incidence of childhood leukaemia in areas close to nuclear installations.

Several of the consequences of atmospheric pollution have been noted above. Decreased visibility is one obvious effect. Damage to health, crops and livestock is another. Increased rates of decay in buildings is a third effect. Air pollution is also the cause of acid rain (see chapter 2) and this is now recognized as being responsible for the acidification of lake and river water and the consequent decline in fish and organic life, as well as causing the deterioration of the health of trees across extensive areas of the Earth (Battarbee *et al.*, 1989; Grayson, 1989; Mason, 1990). Atmospheric pollution is also causing a build-up of carbon dioxide in the air. This is absorbing more of the outgoing heat energy of the planet and seems to be causing a rise in global temperatures. Scientists estimate that the amount of CO_2 in the atmosphere increased by 20% between 1880 and 1980 and that it will rise by a further 20% before 2010. If global temperatures continue to increase because of this greenhouse effect the consequences are almost unimaginable. Partial melting of the polar ice caps and the inevitable rise in sea level that would follow would alone necessitate the removal of whole populations and their economic activities from low-lying areas (Warrick and Farmer, 1990).

Much scientific and even political thought is now being directed at this and other aspects of atmospheric pollution. The United Nation's sponsored Intergovernmental Panel on Climatic Change (IPCC), a group of expert scientists, reported on the greenhouse effect in 1990 and drafted a Framework Convention on the Atmosphere which was discussed by world leaders at the Rio Earth Summit. National and international conferences such as the Noordwijk conference in The Netherlands in November 1989 serve as a platform for airing new information and discussing strategies. The National Environmental Research Council (NERC), an important source of scientific funding in Britain, has identified climatic change as a priority area of research and a new Centre for Climatic Change was established in the UK in 1989.

There are still major uncertainties about the precise causes and especially about the effects of global warming. There are, too, major costs involved in countering existing pollution levels. Several countries including the USA, Russia, Japan and Britain are reluctant to embark upon expensive mitigating programmes that could turn out to be ineffective or unnecessary. Headlines such as 'Britain in new row on global gas limit date' (*The Times*, 7 November 1989), seem set to continue for several more years in spite of a widespread, and growing, acceptance of the dangers of doing nothing.

2 Our changing vegetation

Introduction

The total land area of Earth (excluding Antarctica) is put at 13, 077 million hectares. The total wooded area is estimated at 5228 million hectares or 40%; the area of pasture and rangeland is about 6721 million hectares or 51%. The remainder is made up of rock or barren areas such as sandy deserts (World Resources, 1986). Not all this vegetation cover is natural to its area: some of the wooded areas are plantations of exotic species, for example the radiata pine forests of New Zealand and the rubber plantations of Malaysia; some of the pastures are sown grasses and again New Zealand provides a good example. Although the major part of the Earth's plant cover has been modified to a greater or lesser extent by human agencies, it still, in the main, retains a form which at least has affinities with its natural counterpart. Areas of trees have been most dramatically altered, yet there are still large tracts of forest which are virtually in their natural state, for example the tropical rain forests of Zaire and Brazil. Pastureland and rangeland, in contrast, often show less change but finding areas untouched by human activity (such as commercial ranching and nomadic pastoralism) is very difficult.

People living in developed countries like the United Kingdom, Sweden, France and the United States of America are accustomed to having apparently very precise and accurate data on many aspects of life, not least the natural environment. In fact much of this information is less accurate than it appears, and utilizing it fully often requires additional information which may only be rudimentary. World-wide the accuracy and availability of data is on an even less certain footing. Indeed much of the information relating to the natural environment is little more than a guess. It has been pointed out, for example, that estimates for the world's forested areas range from around 3000 up to about 5000 million hectares or from 23 to 38% of the Earth's land surface (Mather, 1987). Likewise, one estimate of the annual rate of deforestation has been put at 18–20 million hectares per annum (Barney, 1980), a much higher figure than the yearly average of about 10 million hectares presented in the FAO *Production Yearbooks*.

Although it is agreed that most of this deforestation is taking place in the closed tropical broadleaf forests, figures for these areas are among the most unsatisfactory. Thus FAO/UNEP (1982) estimate the annual rate of cutting at 7.1 million hectares, whereas Myers (1980) puts forward estimates of 20–24 million hectares for the same general area. The reasons for such discrepancies are varied. They often result from the use of different definitions of, for example, closed woodlands. They may arise from differences in the methods used to collect the data. They may result from differences in the capacity of countries to collect the data, as well as from the sheer immensity of the task facing some countries. Furthermore, to many of the less developed nations of the world, knowing exactly how much of each natural vegetation type exists within their borders, and how it is changing, must rank relatively low in their priorities.

The value of vegetation

Prior to the emergence of organized human society the Earth's vegetation, in spite of a bewildering mix of species reflecting the interaction of several environmental and biological controls, was arranged in broad zonal belts closely linked with the prevailing world climatic pattern. It was no ornamental cover: it acted as the habitat for the wild life of Earth; it was a key factor in determining the precise gaseous composition of the atmosphere; by means of transpiration the vegetation cover was a major influence upon the amount of water vapour in the atmosphere; via its colour it had a major influence upon the albedo and hence world temperatures. More than this, by growing between the ground and the atmosphere it acted as a major inhibitor of soil erosion, and because it was a major source of humus and soil nutrients, especially nitrogen, it was a major contributor to soil fertility. In addition, the organic acids created during the breakdown phase greatly enhanced the weathering process.

With the emergence of the human species, an economic value had to be added to the above list, for vegetation provides shelter, timber, fuelwood, crops and medicines as well as industrial products such as paper. Perhaps, too, the natural vegetation plays a role in the psyche of *Homo sapiens*. Just as music may in some people inspire changes of mood, or a great painting or outstanding architecture touch hidden sensibilities, so too may a visit to a primeval forest or rangeland touch the spirit.

Vegetation change

The natural vegetation is in a near-continuous state of change produced by evolutionary forces as well as environmental developments. Evidence for this is found in the fossil record, and through the technique of pollen analysis very detailed changes are now recognized, especially those that have occurred in the last 2 million years. These evolutionary and environmentally induced changes continue to the present day but now, additionally, change is produced by human agency. This last change takes many forms. It may be geographic, where a species expands its range when introduced to a new area, for example the flowering cherry (*Prunus*), which was formerly limited to East Asia. It may be botanic in the sense that plant breeding may produce cultivars, for example wheat and barley. It may be economic in the sense that one type of vegetation is replaced by another more valuable form or more frequently that the vegetation is utilized for economic purposes such as grazing, or timber and wood production.

The consequence of this human action is that the natural vegetation is not only subject to change, it is also under threat to a degree that surpasses even that imposed upon it by the onset of the Quaternary glaciations. Then, some extinctions occurred and widespread latitudinal displacement took place, but the overall result was an adjustment to the changing conditions. The new changes are occurring at an unprecedented rate and in response to what is largely a non-environmental challenge. As a result the natural vegetation faces what amounts to an external threat. Under the natural process of adjustment one natural form was replaced by another. Reversion was possible. Under the threat imposed by *Homo sapiens*, so great may be the changes that reversion might be impossible even after some catastrophe had engulfed the human species. Tenacious as the natural vegetation may be (Rackham, 1989), there is at the moment more than a hint of a permanent loss of natural habitat.

Reasons for, and causes of, change

The basic reasons for changing and utilizing the natural vegetation are to provide more food for the ever-expanding world population, now put at over 5000 million, to provide energy particularly as fuelwood and to enhance the living standards of the more affluent members of the world community. Perhaps one should distinguish between deliberate change to the natural vegetation and inadvertent or accidental changes, and between whether the consequences are, in human time scales, long-term or short-term, irreversible or reversible (fig. 4).

While people pursued a nomadic existence, either of the shifting agriculture type associated with the tropical forest areas or as nomadic pastoralists as in Asiatic Russia, permanent damage to the vegetation was slight as long as population numbers remained low. Under these circumstances a return to the climatic climax vegetation was quite possible, if unlikely, when the human pressures were removed, even though for many decades botanical surveys might reveal the past interference through modification to the variety and proportions of species present.

Rising population numbers has meant that pressure on the natural vegetation from non-sedentary peoples has increased. For naturally wooded areas only two options are open to these people: either virgin forest has to be cleared and encompassed within their economic system or the return period to existing sites must be reduced. The latter has the effect of interrupting the succession to a climax vegetation at an earlier stage and leads, if repeated, to the formation of a secondary forest type, distinct botanically, visually and ecologically, which will take much longer to return to a true climax if it is ever given the chance to do so. This slash-and-burn type of shifting agriculture, once condemned as highly destructive, is now viewed more sympathetically by environmentalists as the damage wrought by less sensitive modern farming systems becomes apparent.

Once permanent settlements have been founded and gradual population growth established, the need for an assured food supply arises and clearance of the natural vegetation for cropland, and sometimes pastureland, tends to be more complete and long lasting. The clearance of vegetation in Britain, so skilfully demonstrated by Darby (1951) and Rackham (1986) and considered

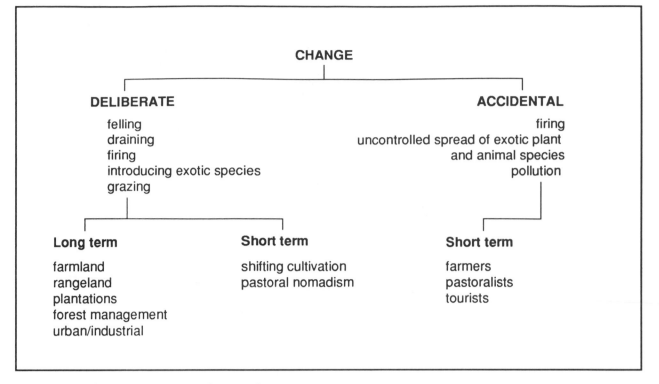

Figure 4   Causes and results of vegetation change.

more fully in a later section, is a good example, but because it has been going on for over 3500 years a complete record is not possible. This is typical of much of western Europe and the Mediterranean lands (Thurgood, 1981).

The clearances associated with the spread of colonists into New World temperate lands took place at a later date and are often recorded in much greater detail. In New Zealand, the dramatic decline in the native vegetation dates only from 1840 with the arrival of the first colonists from Britain. (The indigenous Maoris had had only a modest impact in the previous 1500 years.) Because settlement was relatively orderly the spread of the agricultural frontier and the consequent retreat of the native vegetation is known in some detail, as table 3 and the maps in figure 5 show.

In recent years the main agricultural frontier has been pushed into the areas of tropical rain forest. Three factors are now thought to be the most widespread and important causes of loss of this rain forest habitat and beside them losses to cities, towns, villages, roads and even timber companies are quite small. The first is the need to provide food for a rapidly growing population. The second is to provide land for the landless on which they might eke out a near self-sufficient existence. The third is to provide land for multi-national

Table 3   Area (ha) of occupied land in New Zealand 1881–1961

1881	6,154,147
1891	7,850,072
1901	14,128,520
1911	16,284,146
1921	17,623,131
1931	17,498,820
1941	17,356,672
1951	17,465,029
1961	17,671,690

Source: NZ Year Books

companies on which they can carry out large-scale, low-cost agribusinesses. The second of these factors often leads to additional forest losses via illegal felling and clearing when the initial peasant settlement schemes have failed, as has occurred in both Brazil and Indonesia (Madeley, 1988).

The permanence of such changes seems established until we look at the many examples of land abandonment and its subsequent recolonization by natural vegetation. Large areas in the Upper Wanganui catchment area in New Zealand which were cleared in the 1920s have reverted to secondary forest (Cumberland, 1981). Extensive terraced hill-slopes in Mediterranean France now support a maquis dominated by the

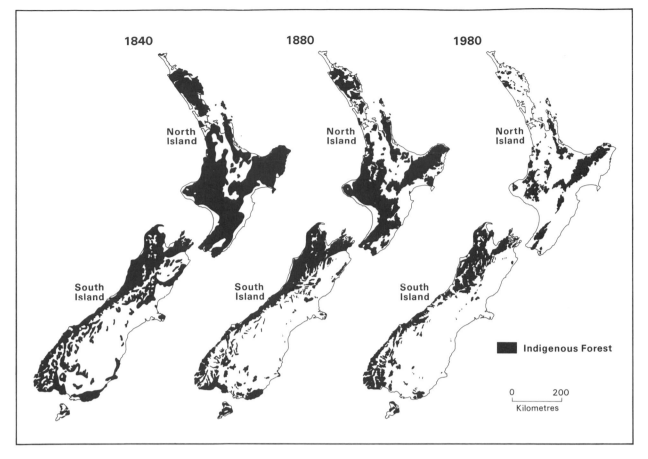

Figure 5   Indigenous forest in New Zealand between 1840 and 1980.
Source: NZ Dept of Conservation; Ward (1976)

holm oak (*Quercus ilex*) instead of the vines, olives and pastures of the 1860s. Even in Britain good examples occur. Documentary evidence in the form of photographs taken in the 1920s of the steep chalkland slopes overlooking Princes Risborough, Buckinghamshire, shows quite clearly that sheep grazing occurred from the clay vale right up to the plateau top (Smith, 1980). Today, much of the same area is a dense thicket of young beech trees, whitebeam and hawthorn. At the time of writing, implementation of the UK government set-aside scheme, whereby farmers are to be paid not to produce farm products from specified areas, seems likely to produce modern examples of recolonization by natural vegetation.

Natural vegetation can be of direct use and hence worth utilizing, preserving, or conserving. Trees and shrubs may be used for timber and energy (firewood, charcoal), rangelands may be grazed, peat may be used as a fuel. The vegetation may have an important role to play as an erosion control or as part of a broader ecological system. The degree of human interference can range from zero in a totally protected area to total clearance in the case of some forestry practices, or poor land management.

There still exist large tracts of forest, particularly in the boreal coniferous zone and in the tropical rain forest areas, that are not exploited for human use, though they may be at some future date. Other areas are actually protected against human use except, in the most stringent cases, for biological research and more generally for recreation. In such cases the decision to protect and then do nothing is a positive act. It means that one is prepared to accept natural change since the vegetation is a dynamic, developing system. Some of the very largest North American national parks come into this category. More often, protected areas are under some degree of active management. This may take the form of culling excess animals deemed to be damaging the vegetation, or perhaps developing a system of regular controlled burning to reduce the danger of major fires and encourage vegetation stability (Pyne, 1982; Malanson, 1985). Another minimal use in protected areas might be to allow one or two specific species to be felled for a designated purpose. In New Zealand, for example, large kauri trees (*Agathis australis*) are occasionally felled in the protected Waipoua forest for ceremonial use by the Maori people.

Commercial exploitation almost always involves much greater disturbance. At one extreme there is the removal of selected timber trees. This system was formerly quite widespread in the tropical rain forests as shown by the removal of teak, using elephants, in Thailand. With such a low percentage of the natural trees cut, and without mechanized extraction methods, only slight damage and change occurred. The modern forestry technique of salvage logging using helicopters to lift out naturally fallen trees is broadly similar but by itself is quite uneconomic.

Today the search for greater profitability as well as quantity means almost always that a far higher percentage of the merchantable trees has to be cut, and they must be extracted mechanically. In theory, if undertaken on a sound ecological/ management basis it should be possible to crop the forest in perpetuity, much as some medieval forests which now form the ancient woodlands of Britain were cropped, for example Hatfield Forest, near Bishop's Stortford, Essex (Rackham, 1989). In practice, things are usually rather different. To be an economic proposition the minimum percentage of timber to be removed is set at between 15% and 40% of the merchantable trees. However, felling large trees causes damage to adjacent trees, the slash produced encourages weed species rather than commercially useful seedlings, and extracting logs by crawler tractor can so damage the roots of other trees that their growth is reduced or terminated. In addition, the opening-up of the forest greatly increases the possibility of windthrow damage. Nor are the trees the most fragile members of the total ecosystem. Disturbance may drive out vulnerable bird and animal species that assist pollination and seedling establishment. In many countries subsequent clearance by squatters following the timber roads into the forest is not uncommon.

Sustained yield management projects using modern techniques have rarely been in operation long enough to show if they can be truly successful. Indeed, several past logging studies show that initial claims (designed to allay the fears of conservationists) have been highly optimistic. In New Zealand, logging trials have shown that one 30% removal of timber resulted in almost 75% of the ground being disturbed whereas another caused only a 33% disturbance (Herbert and Beveridge, 1977; Beveridge and Herbert, 1978). What is emerging from the trials is the fact that results are both highly variable and, at present,

largely unpredictable simply because the interactions between the components of the ecosystem are almost always far from being understood.

More serious changes to the vegetation occur where logging uses the technique of 'mining' an area for all the suitable timber trees. This technique has been widespread in the tropics, in boreal forests, and in the moist lowland forests of New Zealand, where stands of mixed age and species composition are common. It leaves a despoiled vegetation cover lacking many botanical components, a skewed age distribution and a depleted forest structure. Recovery from this type of action is usually very slow. Forest around Auckland, New Zealand, cut more than a hundred years ago, is still far from its natural condition. It will take several more centuries before mature and old-aged trees again form an integral part of the community. In other areas changes to the soil as a result of felling mean that a return to the pre-existing state will be delayed even longer. The 'pakihi' soils of the West Coast, New Zealand, illustrate this. Since logging took place 80 years ago waterlogging and iron pan formation have created very difficult soils on which only fern and poor grasses thrive. In practice, in most areas the result of this type of forestry is the conversion of the land to farmland.

The ultimate devastation occurs when clear-felling takes place. This has been a feature of areas of coniferous forest for many years because of their simple age and species composition. The island of Vancouver, British Columbia, Canada, and areas within the former Soviet Union (Barr and Braden, 1987) provide striking examples. However, in the past 25 years advances in technology have allowed, via the chipmill, a greater range of timbers to be used. As a result, clear-felling has spread into areas of mixed stands in the tropical rain forests and elsewhere. Again conversion to agricultural land often follows, although plantation forestry may occur.

Changes to the vegetation also result from the policy of enrichment. In this case, an area, after more or less severe logging, is cleared of the slash and replanted (enriched) with seedling timber trees. Whilst these may be native species, more often they are faster-growing exotic species. Fast-growing eucalyptus species have been used quite widely for this purpose in parts of East Africa and New Zealand. In practice, this compromise of

Plate 1 Kaingaroa Forest, Volcanic Plateau, North Island, New Zealand. Clear felling of radiata pine. Each compartment is in the order of 30–40 hectares. The staggered nature of the cutting enables replanting to take place over a series of years thereby producing plantations of variable age. Most of these trees were planted in the early 1930s.
Photo: NZ Forest Corporation

introducing fast-growing alien species rarely satisfies either the conservationists or foresters since less timber is produced than if the whole area has been clear-felled and replanted entirely in exotics, while the natural state of the forest is compromised.

Plantation forestry represents an entirely human-made vegetation system. It is now widespread. Productivity from plantations is high and cropping is easy. Hence, if carefully implemented, it can reduce demand upon, and so help conserve, the natural forests. The widespread use of plantation forestry in the moist tropics offers some hope to the remaining rain forests, but the maturity time is about fifty years, suitable land is not always readily available, and demand always seems to increase.

There is, however, opposition to plantation forests. In New Zealand, massive plantings dominated by the radiata pine (native to California) have occurred on the Volcanic Plateau in Central North Island. Plantings began after the First World War and expanded during the depression years. Initially, scrubland, poor-quality pastureland and cut-over forests were used. Regular plantings have continued to the present and these non-native forests now form the basis of a major timber and timber processing (paper) export industry, contributing more than 10% by value of all New Zealand's exports. However, demand has far outstripped supply and the plantations have spread onto previously untouched native forests, to the

dismay of conservationists. This led to a major confrontation between conservationists and the government (the landowner) in the 1970s which was eventually resolved in favour of the conservationists but only after all but the last few remaining native forests had been affected.

In Britain, Forestry Commission plantations are often criticized by recreation organizations. What is seen as part of the 'chocolate box' scenery of Switzerland is viewed very differently if it is transferred to mid-Wales, and recently there have been vociferous protests against the draining and planting of conifers on the 'flow' country of north Scotland. Whether the bog vegetation of the 'flows' is truly natural, or the result of earlier activity by settlers, is not altogether clear, yet the fact remains that the current programme, if unchecked, will substantially alter the vegetation over a wide area and have consequences for the broader ecology of the area.

Agriculture and forestry are two major direct causes of change to the natural environment but inadvertent human action has also brought change. Two examples of this are the damaging effect of introducing alien species as in New Zealand, and atmospheric pollution.

Vegetation and alien species

New Zealand is an isolated island group in the South-West Pacific, distinguished by a native mammalian fauna limited to two species of bat, and a number of small reptiles – some skinks and geckos, and, most notably, the tuatara. The Maoris colonized the country about 1500 years ago and introduced a species of rat and a dog. In contrast, the Europeans who arrived in increasing numbers after 1840 introduced a 'Noah's Ark' of animals, birds and plants. Some of the animals browsed or grazed the lush native vegetation. Among these were the goat, thar, deer, possum, rabbit and hare as well as feral sheep and cattle. Other animals such as feral cats, the European rat and stoats and weasels destroyed the native birds and their eggs, thereby modifying an important seed dispersal mechanism. In some localities introduced plant species have radically altered the vegetation. Among the plants that pose serious problems are gorse, broom, bramble and briar, which have overrun much scrubland and grassland. More recently, the spread of European clematis, (*Clematis vitalba*) has occurred. With its prolific growth, it is now stifling the regrowth of secondary woodland and scrubland in many areas (Ryan, 1985).

Noxious plants are often introduced species. *Rhododendron ponticum*, which is causing widespread concern in areas of North Wales (Tabbush and Williamson, 1987), is a good example from Britain. The spread of bracken *(Pteridium aquilinum)* on many upland moors serves to illustrate how long-established species can change their status (Taylor, 1989).

This type of accidental modification does not have the dramatic impact of clearing for farming and forestry. Rather, it acts slowly from within. Saplings and seedlings are eaten out, thereby producing an ageing forest which in 200 to 300 years must consist of overmature and ageing trees much as the famous Tripoli grove of Lebanon cedars does. Some species are preferentially eaten, altering the species composition, and as gaps appear due to windthrow aged trees are not replaced. Without a dense understorey windthrow becomes more frequent as windspeeds increase.

Fortunately the control of most large noxious animals, although expensive, is possible, even if total eradication is unlikely. Shooting, poisoning, gassing and trapping are four methods available and if targeted at specific areas can have some success. By these means deer, rabbits and goats are less of a threat in New Zealand than they were. In contrast the possum, a nocturnal animal introduced into New Zealand from Australia, is equally at home in pristine forest or suburban garden and is consequently becoming an increasingly serious problem (Cowan *et al.*, 1985; James, 1990). Possum numbers have increased dramatically over the past twenty years and they are now causing considerable damage and death to mature trees by eating the growth tips.

Eradicating or even reducing the smaller carnivorous and omnivorous animals that have had such a devastating effect on the native birds of New Zealand is both more difficult technically and more problematic economically. At present eradication programmes can only be considered for small offshore islands because of the costs involved.

The control of noxious plants is in some senses more difficult than controlling animal populations.

At present effective herbicides are rarely specific to one particular species, and spraying, for example with Agent Orange as was done in Vietnam, risks killing desirable and undesirable plants alike. One alternative is to grub out the unwanted plants but except in special circumstances this is usually impracticable. Hand cutting often results in vigorous regrowth, while if biological control is used the risks involved are high. Solutions to these problems remain to be found.

Vegetation and atmospheric pollution

Inadvertent changes to the natural vegetation are also caused by the effects of atmospheric pollution, which in recent years has received wide publicity because of the effects of acid rain (Mason, 1990). There are well documented instances of this dating back many years. Atmospheric pollution from the metallurgical industries at Swansea, South Wales, were responsible for vegetation damage in the area after 1850 by causing the gradual death of many established plants and inhibiting the regrowth of all but a few tolerant species (Balchin, 1971). The dangers of acid rain were first described more than two decades ago. Now, clear, visible signs of damage have appeared in a variety of natural situations in countries as diverse as Switzerland, West Germany, Britain, Sweden, Norway, Finland, Canada and the USA. In these areas not only are many lakes and rivers now unable to support fish-life and the food chains dependent on it because of the increasing acidity of the water, but trees, both deciduous and coniferous, are also exhibiting signs of stress, with the appearance of dead and dying branches (Tomlinson, 1983; Halford, 1986; Innes, 1989; Park, 1990).

The regional distribution of the damage indicates that air pollution is the primary cause and acid rain is the particular agent. It must be recognized however, that the term acid rain is a very general one. There are many types of atmospheric pollutant and it follows that there must be many different chemical reactions. Thus the acid rain damaging the woodlands near Gatwick airport just outside London derives from kerosene, whereas elsewhere emissions from coal-fired power stations have been highlighted as a major pollutant. It also follows that while there is a general problem associated with acid rain, there will be important local variations in its effects and intensity.

An understanding of the biochemical changes caused by pollutants is gradually emerging (Ulrich, 1983; Bredemeier, 1989). For example, study of the effect of sulphate pollutants on tree growth suggests a four-phase sequence of changes. In phase one the main pollutants actually fertilize the soil causing trees to grow faster for a time. In phase two the ability of the soil to neutralize acidic additives is eventually overcome by the cumulative effects of many years of acidic deposition. In phase three the accumulated and continually added sulphates now combine with the calcium, magnesium and other nutrients and leach them out leaving an acidic soil. It is suggested that the sulphates also react with the organic compounds in the soil which in natural conditions bond large quantities of aluminium (Al) against leaching. At a pH of 4.2 this bonding breaks down and the Al is released in toxic quantities. When the accumulated Al exceeds the amount of calcium in the soil Al toxicity begins to prevent cell division, impair water transport and modify the trees' defence mechanisms, making them more susceptible to disease. At this stage (phase four) trees start to die.

Given the above, different soils will nevertheless respond at different speeds, the tolerance of tree species will vary, tolerance within a single species will vary with the age of the tree, and trees protected by a thick snow cover for a long period may be less vulnerable than others. There are therefore many reasons why trees in one area may be damaged by acid rain while others remain apparently immune.

Solving the problem is difficult, not least because the atmosphere is not nation-specific. The widely dispersed pollution from the Chernobyl nuclear accident showed this extremely clearly. International agreement is, therefore, a prerequisite and in Europe's case this must involve not only agreement between the countries of Western Europe but also between these countries and the former Eastern bloc nations such as Hungary, Poland, Czechoslovakia and East Germany.

Desertification

Changes to the natural vegetation result in the loss of natural habitats, the extinction of species, the diminution of the gene pool, as well as local and even global climatic changes. They also lead to increased soil erosion with the possible result of desertification.

The pressures on the rangelands of the Third World countries have become especially intense since medical advances cut the death rate with consequent increases in the population. This has coincided in recent years with several abnormally dry years. The combined effects have encouraged the encroachment of the desert, a process called desertification. However, the relationship between overuse of pasture and scrub, dieback of vegetation, drought and famine is but part of a wider linkage system involving the natural environment plus population numbers, land-holding policies, political stability, political ideology and other factors (Blaikie, 1985).

As noted earlier, rangelands and grasslands cover a larger area of Earth today than forests do. Utilization of rangelands tends to provoke much less attention than the destruction of forest does, yet because large populations are dependent upon them (30 to 40 million nomadic people in developing countries alone), adverse changes to this natural vegetation type have been responsible for untold misery for millions of people as the recent famines in Ethiopia and the Sahel region of sub-Saharan Africa testify.

The productivity of the rangelands is well below its ecological potential because of human intervention. In the USA, of 883 million hectares of rangeland only 32% is considered to be in good condition, 28% is considered fair, 28% poor and 12% in very poor condition (US Forest Service, 1980). In Africa, where there are 1945 million hectares of rangeland, surveys by United Nations' officials record very few areas in good condition. Usually poor or very poor conditions prevail. Comments for Somalia indicate that deterioration is accelerating; for Sudan deterioration and desertification are accelerating; for Zambia there is a presumed downward trend and in Uganda there is much irreversible erosion (World Resources, 1986).

The human impact takes several forms. At one extreme the rangeland is converted to cropland to provide subsistence food for large and rapidly growing populations or to provide cash crops for export to assist balance-of-payment problems. At the other extreme, light grazing by herds of nomads may be all that takes place (United Nations, 1977). However, in many areas heavy grazing by cattle and sheep is widespread and associated with this is the extensive use of fire to improve the feed quality, reduce animal disease and improve access for cattle farmers. Unless this grazing is carefully controlled, overgrazing and overburning occur, resulting in deterioration of the pasture. In technologically advanced countries such as Australia and New Zealand significant areas of natural grassland have been modified and in some cases eradicated by oversowing with exotic species and by applying heavy doses of fertilizers. In many areas the cutting of scrub vegetation for fuel is very important. This is particularly true in sub-Saharan Africa.

Overgrazing and associated land management practices such as burning are the main causes of pasture deterioration. This deterioration is exacerbated by factors inherent in the system of pastoralism. Domesticated grazing animals, in comparison with their native counterparts, are often heavier, larger beasts whose hooves do more damage to the soil. They are usually much more selective in their choice of food, thereby encouraging the spread of weed species. Above all, by concentrating on just one or two types of grazing animals only a uniform type of grazing occurs, whereas in the natural state, notably in Africa, the annual ordered migration of herds means that successive waves of different species crop the vegetation, some browsing, some nibbling, thereby producing a balanced use.

In the past decade developments in pastoralism suggest that some notice is being taken of this, together with the fact that it is now known that wild animals are usually more efficient than domestic ones at converting food to weight. In Peru, for example, where use of grasslands high in the Andes for sheep and cattle grazing has led to serious vegetation deterioration and soil erosion, there are a growing number of schemes in which the native vicuna has been introduced into the pastoral system. This light, small-hooved animal not only causes less damage to the soil but also eats a much wider variety of species than the sheep do. It is therefore ecologically less damaging and it can provide wool and meat at a cost that makes economic sense (Bernhardson, 1986).

Comparable developments are occurring in Zambia and Zimbabwe, where pilot schemes have been set up in which domesticated herd numbers have been reduced and native species encouraged (WWF News, 1987). Again the aim is to achieve a balanced ecology. In this case the income from hunting is an important element in the economic equation, a situation which raises difficult ethical problems.

Fuelwood

The amount of wood used as fuel, either directly or as charcoal, is put at approximately 1.7 million cubic metres per annum (FAO, 1985). This amounts to rather more than half of the total timber and wood cut annually. It provides the energy source for the needs of over one-third (2.7 billion) of the world's population. In some countries, notably Nepal, Mali, Rwanda, Tanzania, Upper Volta, Ethiopia, Chad and the Central African Republic, wood provides more than 90% of the total energy consumption (Hall et al., 1982). Always in short supply in some areas, firewood in 63 countries is now being cut faster than it can grow back. This is affecting 1.5 billion people (FAO, 1985). Projections suggest that by the year 2000 this figure will have risen to 2.4 billion people (Eckholm et al., 1984).

The effect that this is having on the vegetation is difficult to gauge. Undoubtedly in some areas it is leading to or has led to the depletion of forest areas. This is particularly true where commercial cutting to supply urban markets has taken place. Examples include the area around Kharagpur in West Bengal, Kano in northern Nigeria and along the Sénégal river (Eckholm et al., 1984). However, in rural areas much of the fuelwood is gathered from areas outside designated forests, mainly from trees and shrubs dotted about the farming landscape. In such circumstances the natural vegetation has already undergone severe modification.

Where the wood supply is plentiful dead wood is preferred – it is dry, burns well and is lighter to carry. In these circumstances, although branches may be lopped off, whole trees are rarely felled solely to provide fuel. As demand increases the first reaction is to extend the area of collection, thereby preserving the wood stock but at a cost in time and effort particularly to the women and children who mostly gather wood. Once this strategy is exhausted the almost inevitable consequence is that the wood stock is overcut and then felled. At this stage alternative sources of fuel have to be used. These include leaves, straw and dung. Not only do these produce an inferior fire (less heat and more smoke), thereby making the essential task of cooking more time-consuming and less pleasant, but through burning they are lost as valuable fertilizers to the farming system. In Nepal, diverting manure from the fields to the stove depresses grain yields by 15% (World Bank,

1984). Expressed another way, it has been calculated that the dung used as household fuel in Ethiopia has a fertilizer value of over £50 million per annum (Newcombe, 1984).

The consequences of depleting the fuelwood stock of an area affect, therefore, both physical and cultural resources. The vegetation itself may be changed from forest to scrub although more often major changes have already been effected through farming practices. On steep slopes cutting can leave the soil unprotected and hence contribute to soil erosion (Tiwari *et al.*, 1986). On gentle slopes already farmed, wood depletion may cause dung to be diverted from the fields to the stoves, thereby leading to a breakdown of soil structures as well as a decline in soil fertility. By this means soil erosion may be encouraged and crop yields diminished.

On the cultural side a growing shortage of fuel-wood diminishes the quality of life of the collectors and stove minders. It may result in fewer hot meals for the whole family or the adoption of meals (often less nutritious) that can be cooked more quickly. In urban areas, where most wood has to be purchased (most is 'free' in rural areas), a growing scarcity means rising prices, and this in a situation where a working-class family may already spend a quarter of its meagre income on fuelwood. Finally it should be noted that the burden does not affect all people equally. Some areas have greater reserves than others. The capacity of trees to regrow varies with the species and the natural conditions. More wealthy people have access to alternative fuel sources. It is the poorest who suffer most.

Local examples of vegetation change

Britain

The remains of leaves, bark, flowers and more especially pollen in Tertiary and Quaternary sediments leave no doubt that for much of the past 30 million years the vegetation of the British Isles has been in a state of constant change. For almost all of this long period these changes can be attributed to natural events such as a changing climate, changing geographic position, developing soil conditions, vegetation dynamics and evolution. However, in the more recent past an additional cause of change has been the spread of human activity.

The effects of the Palaeolithic people, and even of the more sedentary Mesolithic folk, were quite small and generally local, although the remains of charcoal and increases in the pollen from habitation weeds such as nettles and plantains point to the reality of change. One such example comes from near Flixton in the Vale of Pickering, Yorkshire (Cloutman and Smith, 1988).

A more substantial impact becomes identifiable about 5000 years ago, specifically at around what palaeo-botanists term the pollen zone Vlla/Vllb boundary. Many sites of this age occur in Britain (and even more in western Europe where this is referred to as the period of landnam clearances). Most notable among the effects on the vegetation is the decline in elm (*Ulmus*) pollen. One view is that this can be explained by pollarding – the lopping of branches back to the trunk – to provide fodder for the expanding numbers of domestic cattle, and thereby inhibiting flowering and pollen production. An alternative view (Rackham, 1986) explains the decline in terms of a major outbreak of Dutch Elm disease, assisted by pollarding since more young susceptible shoots would be available to the insect pest.

By the late Bronze Age archaeological evidence in the form of stone circles, megaliths and burial mounds points to a thriving population spread from Cornwall to the northern isles. By this time clearing of the land for crops was taking place, as well as a marked opening of the woods through the browsing action of cattle. Experimental archaeology has shown how the tools available at the time could be very effective in clearing the smaller timbers. By the end of the Bronze Age perhaps 50% of the wildwood had been cleared, an astonishing achievement given the available technology.

The succeeding Iron Age, characterized by the many hill forts that are dotted around the country, saw an even more concerted use of the wildwood. To the growing agricultural requirements of the period was added the need for charcoal to smelt the iron ore from which the metal that distinguishes the period was derived. Considerable change occurred in those areas close to iron ore mines such as within the great Wealden forest and in the Forest of Dean. Even so the use of wood for charcoal does not imply total clearance. Large timber trees were not suitable for this purpose and seem likely to have been left; it was the smaller poles which were most useful (Rackham, 1986).

22

The impact of Roman colonization upon the natural vegetation is in need of re-assessment in the light of the greater details of this period that have emerged over the past decade. The period of peace established by the Romans encouraged a rise in population, which in turn required more agricultural land to support it and provide exports. Wood-based energy, largely charcoal, continued to be needed for the improved and enlarged technologies, while for almost the first time, large timbers were required for the prestigious buildings in the growing urban centres such as London, York, Chester and St Albans. In addition the growing network of roads constructed under Roman guidance would have opened up the remaining wildwood as surely as the trans-Amazon highways have opened up the rain forest there since 1965. However, the Romans also clearly understood the economic value of woodland management. They introduced the sweet chestnut (*Castanea sativa*), almost certainly for coppicing (plate 2).

During the unsettled years of the later part of the Roman occupancy and in the years that followed their departure it is possible that some farmland was abandoned and recolonized by the natural vegetation. There is little evidence either from pollen analysis or archaeology to indicate this was widespread. Nor, in general, do the names of Anglo-Saxon settlements established at this time support this view. Woodland place names ending in -ley or -hurst remain uncommon in areas thought to have been agricultural land in the Roman period such as Lincolnshire, south-east Warwickshire, north Oxfordshire and east Gloucestershire. Where common, in known wooded areas such as the Weald and the Chiltern plateau, they seem to indicate the foundation of a settlement within a clearing in the wood rather than the actual felling of trees and subsequent settlement (Rackham, 1986).

The records of the Domesday Book (1086) provide a remarkable snapshot of Britain at that time, and it is evident, as Darby (1951) and Rackham (1986) have shown, that the last vestiges of the wildwood had almost certainly gone by this date. True, large tracts of forest remained in such areas as the Weald, the Chiltern plateau, Sherwood and the New Forest but by 1086 most of it was managed in some form or other and it would have been difficult to walk for more than a few kilometres before coming across a clearing. Using the Domesday Book data as a guide it is suggested that

only 15% of England was wooded in 1086, less than in 1950. This woodland had to provide almost all the energy needs of the country. It could do this only on a sustained yield basis. Woodland management had become a major support of the economy of the country.

In spite of the growing population and the expansion of towns and industries the amount of woodland in Britain appears to have remained relatively constant over the next 800 years. Indeed records indicate that many of the woods were a persistent feature of the landscape in spite of their intensive use. Today these are the so-called ancient woodlands. They are characterized by a rich and varied flora. The Bradfield Woods, Suffolk, for example, support about 350 species. Hatfield Forest (plate 2) in north-west Essex is another ancient woodland. It is especially important as it remains virtually intact as an example of a medieval wood. Most of the remaining ancient woodlands cover only a few hectares and more have been lost since 1950 than in the previous 400 years (Rackham, 1980; 1989).

Use of these woodlands has undoubtedly modified the vegetation but what remains lies much closer to

Plate 2 Coppiced woodland, Hatfield Forest, Essex. Coppicing and the related pollarding are techniques of woodland management formerly widely practised in Britain and western Europe. The technique provided a sustained yield of wood suitable for fuel, charcoal and many agricultural and building purposes. The techniques fell into disuse as non-renewable resources became widely available and have only recently been revived, so far mainly as a conservation measure since many of these coppices at least are remnants of ancient woodland. In this photograph the poles are neatly stacked awaiting removal while much of the brushwood is piled around the coppiced stools to prevent deer and rabbits browsing on the new regrowth shoots. An alternative technique is to use some of the poles and the brush to construct a fence around the whole area.

Plate 3 Burnt Heath, Thursley Common, Surrey. On sandy acid soils in lowland areas the native woodland was often cleared and replaced by a rough grazing system that encouraged the spread of heathland plants. In recent years competing land-use claims for this low-value land has led to its dramatic reduction in area. Conserving lowland heath requires active management since it easily reverts to birch and pinewood. Careful use of fire is one technique that can enhance the growth of heather and gorse while at the same time killing tree seedlings. Accidental fires, caused by discarded cigarette ends, bonfire sparks, etc, such as this one, may result in serious damage to the heathland ecology.

the natural vegetation than the vegetation of the planted woodlands does. There are many examples of the latter, most of which post-date the 18th century. Early plantings between 1780 and 1850 were often of the native oak (*Quercus robur*) to take advantage of the requirements of the tanning industry. Many of today's small but valued oak woods remain following the collapse of this trade. Since the First World War economic factors have encouraged the planting of quick-growing conifers. Many ancient woodlands were lost this way. But large areas, previously unwooded, have also been coniferized. Central Wales and the Border counties provide large-scale examples. Mainly by this means the wooded area of Britain has actually increased since 1950.

The natural vegetation of Britain is essentially mixed deciduous woodland. However, as a result of human interference other distinct vegetation types have been created over the years which are now regarded as valued quasi-natural habitats. The lowland heaths are one example (plate 3). Created by clearing the woodland and maintained by a specific type of farming and land use, these heathlands reached their greatest extent in the 17th and 18th centuries. Changing farming methods and land values have seen many of these areas

ploughed up or planted with conifers and, in the case of heathland near cities, built upon. Dorset has lost 80% of its heathland since 1811 and of the 10,000 ha remaining in 1960 almost 50% had been lost by 1980 (Moore, 1962).

The Mediterranean

The Mediterranean region contrasts with Britain in many ways as far as the interaction between *Homo sapiens* and the vegetation is concerned. Just three points will be noted here. First, the natural environment is much more prone to fire damage than the moist deciduous woodlands of Britain. Second, many areas have been settled for much longer. Third, a peasant-based, pastoral economy has been an enduring feature of many areas.

Pollen remains are much less common in the drier lands of the Mediterranean basin than in Britain and consequently the detailed vegetation history is less well known. Even so, enough has been researched to indicate that over the Quaternary period as a whole vegetation change has been a continuing theme. Identifying the Mediterranean wildwood is not, however, easy. Several writers have suggested that the better-watered areas supported a dry schlerophyllous woodland characterized by evergreen oaks (*Quercus ilex*), pine species (*Pinus halepensis*), or mixtures of the two (Polunin and Huxley, 1965; Harant and Jarry, 1967). Thurgood (1981) has even suggested that much of the drier eastern Mediterranean such as the Levant – Lebanon, Syria and Palestine – and even parts of Egypt, once supported widespread forests of this type. Archaeological evidence, as well as pictorial and documentary data, point in this direction.

Today much of the Mediterranean region is not wooded. It can be argued that small but important changes in climate over the past 5000 years have been the most potent factor in the deforestation of the area, but the weight of evidence now suggests that human interference has been the major cause. To the classical civilizations of the Near East, trees were both an important energy source and provided timber. Much of the early trade of Egypt was with the Lebanon and as early as 2500–2300 BC Egyptian papyri start reporting a shortage of cedar wood and the wood oil and resin used in embalming (Thurgood, 1981). Such shortages must have been purely relative since timber exports from the Lebanon continued for another

3000 years. However, this trade in timber, the growing peasant population and the destruction of woodland led to the progressive clearance of the natural vegetation throughout the area. In the Lebanon, for example, three-quarters of the country is now classed as grazing or waste land (one-quarter is under cultivation). The famed cedars, once widespread over some 80,000 hectares at between 1500 m and 2400 m, are now reduced to 12 limited stands. The best known, the Tripoli grove, now comprises 43 old large trees and about 400 younger ones, but few if any seedlings are being established on the bare, trampled soil beneath.

Much of the destruction here and elsewhere in the eastern Mediterranean has been caused by the peasant-based pastoral system of agriculture. This system has persisted for a variety of reasons, social and political, as well as physical. The flocks of sheep and goats are a familiar sight. They are present in very high absolute numbers and at a high stocking rate. Writing of the Lebanon mountains an FAO report (1961) comments 'so heavy is goat grazing . . . that the flocks have already consumed nearly all forms of vegetation within reach. The shepherds, unperturbed, have therefore resorted to felling the last remnants of high forest in order to satisfy the empty bellies of their ravenous flocks.' In contrast, in the western Mediterranean, especially in France, the rural peasant has largely vanished and very strict controls exist on the number of goats that may be kept.

Closely associated with browsing by flocks of goats and sheep is the firing of the vegetation to produce an early nutritious feed. Again, in France, stringent fire regulations are in operation. Elsewhere they are more lax or non-existent. However, the vegetation is highly susceptible to fires and accidental fires are very common throughout the whole area. In France many fires are associated with recreational activities such as camping and picnicking (Hull, 1986). One further cause of fire needs to be mentioned, that of a tactic in warfare. Extensive areas of the wooded Troödos massif in Cyprus were fired during the hostilities between the Greek and Turkish communities in the 1970s. Large areas of Mediterranean France were fired by the Germans in the Second World War. Many earlier conflicts used the same technique. The result was to impoverish and diminish the woodlands and scrubland and to extend the garrigue (a community of low, scattered, often spiny and aromatic shrubs) and the

steppe (a species-poor community, mostly made up of grasses).

The effect of all this human activity plus the clearance of land for agriculture has been to create a vegetation cover no more natural than that of Britain. However, there is much more uncultivated vegetation around. The peasant economy of the eastern Mediterranean means that scrubland, in the form of garrigue or the more degraded steppe, is widespread. The great shift away from the peasant economy in France, and to a lesser extent in Italy and in Spain, has led to rural depopulation and the abandonment of much of the land. In these countries large areas of garrigue or the more densely vegetated maquis occur. Many formerly terraced slopes are now covered with scrub and recolonizing woodland. Extensive areas in the south of France have also been replanted for forestry purposes.

New Zealand

If the human influence upon the vegetation of Britain and the Mediterranean area has been profound, in New Zealand it has been flagrant. Here burnt and burning stumps remind one of the vegetation that was; here the chainsaw screams in the mountain stillness. In fact the human impact has been very complex. This relates partly to the highly idiosyncratic set of natural ecosystems that occur within New Zealand. Situated in the south-west corner of the Pacific Ocean over 1500 km from the nearest landmass, New Zealand is today still relatively isolated. This isolation has persisted through a significant period of geological time. Structural evidence points to the Tasman Sea starting to open 80 million years ago, a process virtually complete after 20 million years (Stevens, 1980). Even before this New Zealand was marginally situated on the great southern landmass of Gondwanaland.

This marginality and subsequent isolation helped to create and preserve a unique ecosystem. Ecologists can draw up a long list of distinctive characteristics. Five of the major features are:

1) The absence of native land mammals apart from the tuatara (*Sphenodon* sp.), species of skink and gecko and two native bats.
2) The occurrence of several species of native birds that are either flightless or have poor powers of flight.
3) The occurrence of a rich variety of trees of the

Plates 4 and 5 *The effects of browsing by a heavy deer population are clearly evident in these two plates. In plate 4 (left), the dense understorey and ground flora of this beech/podocarp/hardwood forest at Puketitiri, Hawkes Bay, New Zealand, can be seen. This contrasts with the almost bare, open character of the forest floor in plate 5 (right) taken in the beech protection forest of the upper Caples valley, South Island, New Zealand.*
Photos: NZ Forest Corporation

Podocarp family, a group with a particularly ancient lineage.

4) The occurrence of a high proportion of endemic species.

5) The development of the vegetation in the absence of major herbivors.

New Zealand has the distinction of being the last large land area to be colonized on a permanent basis. The Polynesians (Maoris) arrived probably only some 1500 years ago, and the Europeans, in large numbers, only 150 years ago. This means that although the history of Maori influences on the vegetation remains a little unsure, the European influence is known in detail. The spread of occupied land has been noted in table 3 and figure 5. Clearance of land for agriculture by felling, burning and draining, coupled with the oversowing of the natural grasses with clover, exotic grasses and the application of fertilizers in large quantities, have been widespread. Change also proceeded at what was, until recently, an unprecedented rate since European occupancy post-dated the start of the Industrial Revolution.

Much of this agricultural land was carved out of the dense forests. For example, 40 Mile Bush near Dannevirke was effectively cleared between 1872

Table 4 Area (ha) of plantation forests in New Zealand, 1921–86

1921	76,000	1956	418,000
1926	105,000	1961	430,000
1931	285,000	1966	480,000
1936	375,000	1971	530,000
1941	392,000	1976	729,000
1946	397,000	1981	888,000
1951	407,000	1986	1,100,000

Source NZ Year Books

and 1900 by the simple expedient of setting fire to it: 'The conflagrations of the autumn burns, when successful, were matched by the unsought fires of a dry summer. The most severe outbreaks ever to purge the region were in January and February 1897 and 1898 when devouring holocausts in the North Wairarapa and on the east coast rolled over thousands of hectares' (Bagnall, 1976).

Much of the forest was first cut over for its timber and then burnt, or simply abandoned. Abandoned land, now over 100 years old, often forms good secondary forest but it is clearly much modified. The Waitakere Hills near Auckland provide a good example.

So great was the cutting by timber companies that by the 1960s few natural areas remained of the once widespread, unique, lowland podocarp-mixed hardwood forests. Intense action by conservationists over the past 25 years finally convinced the New Zealand government of the need to conserve some forests in their natural state and several important forests are now protected (Morton *et al.*, 1984). Thus, unlike in Britain, one can actually visit areas of natural vegetation.

The story of these remaining forests is often one that has involved conflict between foresters and conservationists. This is well illustrated from the West Coast, South Island, forests (Wright, 1980), a case study of which appears on pages 28 and 29.

Even these areas are not entirely safe from human influence for the peculiar nature of the ecosystem has meant that it is especially vulnerable to damage and modification by introduced species of mammals, birds and plants, for example the goat, deer, possums and rabbits; gorse, briar and European clematis.

Concern at the effects of these exotic species was expressed from a very early date. In 1888 the owner of Molesworth, a large farm in South Island, was writing to his farm manager as follows: 'I hope at Xmas to find all the briars grubbed' and again in 1889: 'Re the briars at the Rainbow, [part of the farm] I would like Tudhope to take a contract to destroy them thoroughly, say for £10.00. His boys would do it well.' But they didn't. By 1906 he was writing: 'the Elliot [another part of the farm] I must let go as I cannot afford £1000'. In 1965 briars still threatened 14,000 hectares and by then would cost £84.00 per hectare to clear or in excess of £1 million (McCaskill, 1969).

Examples of action designed to reduce the wasteful destruction of forests include the 1877 Land Act, which set aside large areas of upland forest with a view to minimizing soil erosion on the steep slopes. This was followed by other pieces of legislation such as the 1892 Land Act, the 1894 Tongariro National Park Act and the 1908 Scenery Preservation Act. Even so, destruction continued to such an extent that in 1913 a Royal Commission was established to study the issue. One outcome of this was the formation in 1919 of the New Zealand Forest Service (now Forest Corps). One can argue that by encouraging less wasteful use of the native trees and through initiating a planting programme of high yielding, fast-growing exotic trees (table 4) the speed at which the native forests were being cleared was reduced. However, the Forest Service was not a conservation organisation; its objectives were stricly commercial. Although undoubtedly better forest management occurred, by the mid-1960s the remaining areas of lowland forest had been reduced to crisis proportions. This occurred in spite of much additional legislation relating to forests and scenic preservation.

Now, the modern forestry industry, which forms an important part of the New Zealand economy, is much less wasteful of the timber and utilizes and researches modern techniques of forest management. Techniques used range from salvage logging from environmentally sensitive areas, through sustained yield management extracting between 15 and 40% of the millable timber, to enrichment schemes, to clear-felling followed by total replanting. All alter the natural ecosystem to a greater or lesser extent.

The history of forest exploitation in New Zealand is an example of more than local interest. It shows how difficult it is to conserve forests. New Zealand has over 100 years of legislative history relating to forests and areas of outstanding natural beauty. It has been a country whose timber companies have been essentially local, not outposts of multi-nationals. Since 1919 there has been no pressure to create more agricultural land. It is an affluent country well able to afford the research and management of its forests. It has a highly educated population quite capable of understanding the issues involved. These, and other factors not mentioned, are almost the opposite of the situation found in most Third World countries. Even so, New Zealand's forests stood on the brink of destruction (Searle, 1975).

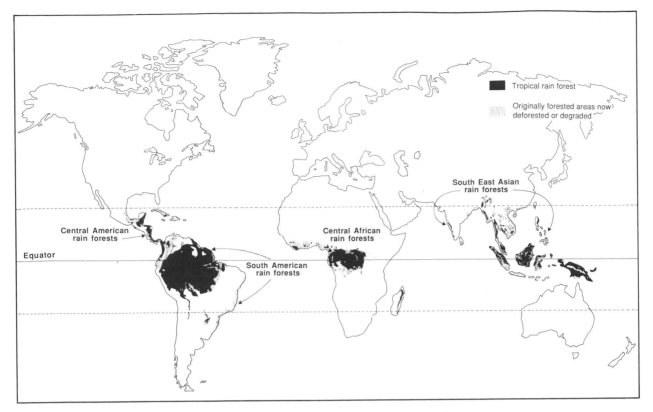

Figure 6 **The distribution of the tropical rain forest today and its pre-20th-century extent.**

Forests in New Zealand illustrate most dramatically the human impact but most other vegetation types have also been modified to some extent. Much of the alpine vegetation has been browsed by introduced deer; most of the natural grassland has been heavily grazed, frequently burnt and often top-dressed with fertilizers. Many sand dune areas have been grazed, or damaged by trail-bikes. Mining schemes, hydroelectric power projects and even pressure from tourists are just some of the pressures that exist upon these other vegetation types.

Brazil

Few conservation topics have aroused so much controversy, passion and publicity in the 1980s as the cutting of the tropical rain forests generally, and those of Amazonia in particular. Proponents of the felling see it as a much needed source of revenue for a debt-ridden nation and the land released as a much needed means of finding land for the landless peasants. Opponents forecast dire local consequences such as soil erosion, and catastrophic global damage via the 'greenhouse' effect. One simple view is that this is one of the last natural wilderness areas on Earth and as such it should be saved.

The majority of informed opinion now believes that these forests are under threat (Barney, 1980). However, obtaining accurate data is difficult for reasons such as the scale of the forests and the reliability of the information. Thus 'guesstimates' forecast that the Brazilian tropical forests will be seriously depleted by the year 2010, 2025 or 2050.

In spite of the lack of accurate figures for the remaining virgin and secondary forest, and the rate at which any type of forest is being cleared, it is evident that the speed of depletion is now very rapid (Mather, 1987). Figure 6 gives some indication of the scale of rain forest clearance.

There are several direct causes of clearance but none would have been nearly so effective had not a series of roads been pushed through Amazonia. These had the effect of vastly increasing the margins of the forest along which incursions could take place. Cutting the trees for timber or wood chips is one important cause of forest depletion. Set against this, forestry industries are reported to have established over 250,000 hectares per year of forest plantations during the decade of the 1970s (Sedjo & Clawson, 1984). The establishment in 1987 of the International Tropical Timber Organisation (ITTO), an institution which bears a United Nations Charter, is a further move which could regulate exploitation in Brazil and elsewhere. To date, however, progress through the ITTO has been slow.

Case study: the West Coast forests' story

The natural forests
The West Coast forests of South Island, New Zealand are composed of two basic elements. One group is represented by what are known as podocarp and mixed hardwood species, the other group by species of southern beech. These represent the warmth-loving species with sub-tropical links, and the cold-tolerant sub-antarctic species respectively. On the West Coast the podocarp and mixed hardwoods are found at the lower levels, often on the fluvio-glacial terraces and moraines up to 500 m above sea level while the beech forests are dominant above this level on the mountain slopes. In many areas at the lower level the two are intermixed in various proportions.

Until very recently the valuable timber trees were limited to the podocarp-hardwood species, especially the rimu and kahikatea. As a result felling was concentrated on lowland areas. Since the lowlands were also the sites for clearance for farmland and were of limited extent, the threat to this ecosystem was intense. It was saved initially by the area's isolation from the rest of New Zealand, and the damp climate (2000 mm or more rain each year). Isolation encouraged the larger timber companies to exploit more accessible forests in the North Island and the climate and isolation made for difficult farming conditions. Removal of the luxuriant forest often initiated a sequence of chemical changes within the soil which resulted in loss of nutrients, pan formation and water-logging. Today these are known as pakihi soils.

Early history
Before 1860 the West Coast forests were effectively untouched by human action. A few trees, the stumps still visible today, had been cut down by Captain Cook at Astronomer's Point in Dusky Sound. Others, doubtless, had been felled by Maoris engaged in collecting greenstone. The rush to the West Coast gold fields in 1864 changed all this. Not only were trees felled for timber for use in the gold-winning process, they were also felled to allow towns to be built and tracks to be cut. Once the tracks to the towns over the Southern Alps had been established, forests began to be replaced by farmland. At the same time small timber companies began to exploit the forest resources, exporting the timber via the coastal ports and, after 1923, by rail via the Otira tunnel to Christchurch.

Early conservation
At first sight, the designation of much of the beech forest covering steep slopes as protection forest, and the establishment of the Fiordland area as a National Park in 1905, might encourage optimism about conservation. However, it was the ecologically more diverse lowland forests that were threatened by the timber companies and farmers and none of these were protected, except for small areas designated scenic or scientific reserves, neither of which had strong legal protection. The formation of the Westland National Park in 1960 again concentrated almost exclusively on the high altitudes.

Modern exploitation
After 1950 better roads, increased demand and more powerful machinery were just three of the factors that led to an increase in the cut from the West Coast forests. Yet, even by the late 1960s, much lowland forest remained, even if some of the finest areas had been destroyed. The position changed dramatically in the 1970s as alternative sources of timber in North Island were cut out, conversion of areas of native species to areas of exotic pines became fashionable, and new uses for trees, notably the export of wood chips, were developed.

Modern conservation
The story of the conservation of the West Coast forests really begins about 1965 with a proposed hydroelectric power scheme at Lake Manapouri in Fiordland; it continues via the battle to save the remaining lowland forests in central North Island and only focuses on the West Coast proper after 1978. The first two events are important as they saw the initial mobilization and organization of a mass conservation movement in New Zealand. The Save Lake Manapouri campaign collected over 264,907 signatures from a (then) total population of under 3 million. The magnitude of the change this produced is hard to over-emphasize. The national government actually modified, by some large measure, a major development scheme. Ten years later a comparable protest saw the government of the day virtually overturn its policy of 50 years towards the

cutting of native species in North Island. With the West Coast forests by now the only large remaining area of state-owned native production forest, the battle lines were drawn up.

Arrayed against the conservationists were the economic, social and even legal arguments of the government. Forestry meant jobs in an area of high unemployment. Forestry exports meant overseas funds at a time of falling farm exports. Contracts already signed with timber companies for 25, 50 and even 100 years had to be honoured. In addition it was claimed that by utilizing modern techniques of timber extraction (techniques only grudgingly adopted after the confrontation over North Island indigenous forests), native forests could be milled without significant damage, and that this, together with the establishment of the State Forest ecological reserves that had occurred in the mid-1970s gave an important measure of protection.

Conservationists in New Zealand were unconvinced by the last arguments and mounted a sustained and vigorous campaign for both more extensive and better protected lowland forests. The weight of this opposition gave it political leverage, its research efforts gave it respectability, and its panache for publicity ensured that the issue was constantly in the news.

Confronted by ever increasing criticism of its policies towards native forests, the government and the NZ Forest Service embarked on a sequence of damage limitation moves. Standards of timber extraction were improved; low-level beech forest was to be substituted for much of the existing podocarp production forest; a logging moratorium was placed on areas zoned as ecological and scientific reserves; internal organizational changes placed greater emphasis on conservation.

Sustained pressure from conservation groups specifically directed at the West Coast forests, and the continued growth of the 'green' movement nationally, finally convinced the government, in 1986, that most of the remaining forests should be protected in some measure. The Paparoa National Park was announced, permanent legal protection was given to 58 ecological and scenic reserves and a North Westland Wildlife Corridor was set aside for reserve protection. In all this totalled 137,000 ha. At the same time zoned production forest was reduced from 292,000 ha to 120,000 ha.

At about the same time a suggestion was made that the Fiordland National Park, together with Mt Aspiring National Park, Mt Cook and Westland National Parks, plus adjacent crown land, such as the Red Hills and state forests of South Westland, should be proposed as a World Heritage site. This proposal again involved decisions to rezone production forest to protected forest (although a moratorium on logging had been applied). In February 1989 a decision to halt felling was taken and in late 1990 the other elements needed for the 2.2 million ha area to go forward as a Heritage site were agreed to.

The West Coast forests' story thus has a happy ending, provided minerals are not found, since at present New Zealand law gives mineral extraction priority over other legislation. Unquestionably much has been saved for future generations, but much has been lost.

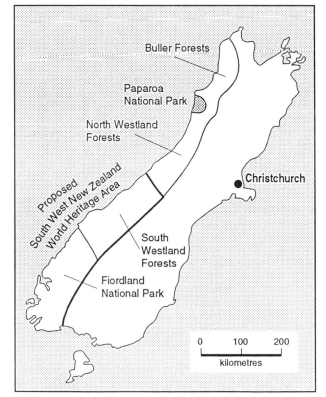

South Island, New Zealand: location of place names mentioned in the text.

Clearing the Amazonian forest for 'colonial' settlements is a second and probably more important cause of destruction. In this case the forest is burnt with only minimal use being made of the available timber. Graphic accounts of these forest fires have appeared in newspapers, journals and on TV. In 1988 alone it is estimated that 40 million hectares of prime virgin forest and pastureland (1% of the total area and almost equal in size to Denmark) were burnt in Amazonia. New measures announced late in 1988 by the Brazilian government were aimed at reducing this figure in the future.

Clearance for large-scale ranching is another cause of deforestation, and one that has particularly angered many conservationists, since much of this destruction has been on behalf of large North American companies seeking cheap hamburger meat with minimum benefits to Brazil. To this depressing list must be added the loss of forest to flooding produced by massive hydroelectric power schemes. To date the completed schemes have been peripheral to the main forest but several schemes are scheduled for Amazonia.

Arriving at an agreed management plan for Amazonia must involve the Brazilian government. It is just as much a political decision to do nothing as it is to pass and enforce legislation. There are some hopeful signs of government action. The Acre Project is one. The State of Acre is located in western Amazonia adjacent to Peru. Forests cover about 95% of the state. Previously isolated, a paved road will soon bisect the state; development will certainly follow. The Brazilian Government (1987) suggested to an ITTO meeting that Acre becomes a commercial-scale test of the proposition that the forests can be managed on a sustained yield basis. To establish and undertake such a project is difficult. Demonstrating its success (if this occurs) must take many years.

There is not universal support for the scheme in Acre (Wheelwright, 1989). On 22 December 1988 Francisco 'Chico' Mendes, rubber tapper, conservationist, participant at international conferences and the most famous inhabitant of Xapuri, was fatally shot, having survived at least five previous attempts on his life. Perhaps the murder of this internationally renowned Brazilian will serve more than anything else to take the conservation issue out of the drawing rooms of Brazil's urban left, out of academic Common Rooms and out of the ecological magazines of non-tropical countries and make it central to Brazil's political development. Meanwhile the current exploitive model is still followed.

Hope for the future

The previous pages have shown that both the forests and rangelands/grasslands of Earth have been, and more importantly are being, utilized by and for the growing human population. In many temperate regions, notably in Britain and western Europe, the almost total destruction of the natural vegetation and its replacement with crops, grassland, managed forests and plantations has on a practical level at least, produced little irreparable damage. It has led to vastly increased productivity in the form of food, wood and timber. It is, however, apparent that in many other areas of the world, for example those countries with a more extreme climate and those with steeper slopes, the application of techniques and attitudes developed in temperate regions may give only short-term gains and end in massive long-term losses. There is, too, more than a hint that in some critical areas the consequences of these modern changes may be both local and world-wide, through changes in world climates and sea levels, for example.

The driving force for these changes has been social and economic. Ironically the driving force for much conservation is also becoming economic. Increasingly it is being suggested that loans to the debt-ridden Third World countries should be conditional upon major conservation programmes being established. Not surprisingly this 'greening' of overseas loans is not viewed with the same enthusiasm in the debtor nations.

Nor do moral arguments provide much comfort. Viewing Earth as a Celestial Ark, one can question whether one species has the right to deny others space to live. Have people in wealthy nations the right to deny some of the world's poorest people the right to try to improve their standard of living, even the right of just living, so that some beast or plant may survive? Similarly one can argue that to destroy much that is currently unknown, misunderstood or valueless, is to deny to future generations the possibility of altered perspectives and economic values. But people are dying *now* through lack of food. Which is more important?

It is the very pace of contemporary change that makes the resolution of these issues so important and so difficult. It is no idle claim that if present trends continue then within the lifespan of present British school-children most of the virgin tropical rain forest will be lost. The weight of evidence encourages a gloomy forecast. Yet there are some pointers to a more positive outcome. Attitudes to the environment are changing rapidly in many developed countries. This should help safeguard their local environment, and if sensitively handled could be used to aid Third World countries.

Within some Third World countries, in spite of appalling obstacles, outstanding efforts are being made to safeguard critical areas. Ironically the first serious test of the new resolve to protect the environment may be in a continent devoid of almost all vegetation – Antarctica. If international agreement to preserve untouched this most isolated and unvegetated of land masses is not forthcoming, hope for other, more populous areas, is slim indeed.

3 Soil and the human impact

Introduction

Soil, no less than vegetation, is an extremely variable resource. One consequence of this is that any detailed classification of soils over a large area involves a long list of names. The US Department of Agriculture (USDA) classification, for example, called Soil Taxonomy, already recognizes more than 16,800 soil series in the United States with more being added all the time. Fortunately, just as one can recognize broad groups of vegetation, such as winter deciduous forest or savanna, so one can identify broad zonal soil groups. Such groups comprise the highest level of the USDA classification, among them spodosols, mollisols, oxisols and aridisols (Brady, 1990). Some of these soils are characterized by deep profiles, others tend to be shallow, some are fertile, others infertile, some are prone to erosion and others are highly stable. These and other variable features testify to their diversity.

The value of soil

The human species is heavily reliant upon plants, crops and, indirectly, pastures for its nutrition. Since these same plants, crops and pastures depend on the soil for their food, soil is of fundamental importance to human well-being. It is important in other ways too. Soil acts as a buffer between the atmosphere and the rocks and sediments beneath. A thick soil cover promotes the infiltration and effectiveness of precipitation as a water resource. A good soil inhibits run-off and reduces flooding. A fertile soil is also a resilient soil and is less prone to soil erosion.

This concept of good and less good soils has long been recognized in many countries and has been reflected in the different price paid per hectare for agricultural land in different areas (Cruickshank, 1972). In the UK, for example, fenland land prices are usually higher per hectare than chalkland land prices. Elsewhere, in areas of conflicting land use claims, highly fertile soils have been retained in agricultural use through Town and Country Planning zoning. Class I land near Hastings and Napier, New Zealand, threatened with industrial development, comes into this category.

The natural vegetation and soil exist in an intimate association, but, just as the vegetation has been altered, so too has the soil. Not all human intervention has been bad. Natural soils can be improved with careful management just as plants can be improved by selective breeding. Yet much of the evidence points in the opposite direction. All too often intervention by agriculturalists and pastoralists has led to reduced fertility, reduced potential and increased soil erosion.

What is soil?

Soil is a dynamic medium, sometimes of extraordinary complexity. Defined here as the medium in which most plants grow, soil is the product of rock and sediment weathering and erosion. At its simplest, rock and sediment weathering produces loose inorganic material and voids. The voids are filled, partially or wholly, with air and water. These three components, inorganic material, air and water, provide the basic ingredients of a chemical broth in which many chemical reactions are continuously taking place. In most cases a further component of the soil is organic matter, dead and alive. This greatly enhances the intensity and range of the chemical reactions, and also contributes strongly to the physical character of the soil.

Soil is dynamic but it is also well ordered. It is this order which makes it possible to provide meaningful, generalized soil descriptions of podzols, chernozems, brown earths, etc. Order is best seen in the division of a vertical section of soil (the soil profile) into more or less distinct layers called horizons. Each soil, indeed each horizon, possesses certain physical and chemical properties. Among the most obvious are (a) texture, a measure of grain size and proportionality, (b) structure, the nature of grain aggregation, (c) chemical composition simply defined on a pH scale from acid to alkaline, and (d) colour as measured against a Munsell soil colour chart. Even considering just these four properties it is possible to grasp something of the range of soil characteristics that can occur, and how easy it is to change the natural state.

One further point should be noted. The rate of soil formation, although variable, is generally slow. There are exceptions, notably where an outside agent causes loose material to be deposited, for example a glacial moraine, a coastal dune, an alluvial deposit or a volcanic ash shower; then, signs of soil formation may emerge quite quickly, but usually a soil derived from the weathering of solid rock has taken thousands if not tens of thousands of years to build up a thickness of a metre or more. Soil, protected by its vegetation cover, is remarkably stable in spite of its lack of strength (it ploughs easily). But once exposed to wind and water erosion, or weakened still further by agricultural practices, soil may be removed rapidly.

Changes to the soil

Once the vegetation has been modified by human actions the soil beneath it is also modified. It is the recognition of this that forms the basis of shifting agriculture in the tropics. Clearing the forest stops almost all the supply of organic matter to the soil. For the first year the reserves in the soil are high and help provide a nutritionally rich soil. Biological processes, leaching in the heavy rainfalls, oxidation, plus the act of cropping remove much of the reserves by the second season and a reduced crop results. The downward spiral continues until after the third or fourth season the plot has to be abandoned and allowed to revegetate to replenish the organic matter.

Technologically advanced cropping and pasture farming bring about many changes in the soil. Deliberate changes are designed to improve the soil conditions. Among these, field drainage by means of mole drains is, perhaps, the least obvious but is extremely widespread in the UK (Robinson *et al.*, 1990). The draining of fen and peat soils by large ditches is also important. The converse of this is irrigating soils.

Adding fertilizers, especially nitrogen, potash and phosphate, but also trace elements, to achieve optimum nutritional levels for specific crops, is a major means of modifying the soil chemistry, as is liming to decrease its acidity. New Zealand provides excellent examples of the use of fertilizers upon its soils. In order to sustain its high-quality pastures 3.6 million hectares of rain-drenched hill country are top-dressed from the air each year and since 1949 over 30 million tonnes of phosphate and lime have been dropped. Curiously, in some areas these fertilizers did not improve conditions until, in 1931, it was discovered that a cobalt deficiency was the underlying cause of low productivity. Once this was added to the mixture flock and herd health and growth improved significantly.

Most agricultural practices, however, also bring about inadvertent changes to the soil. Destruction of the natural vegetation and ploughing often combine to greatly change both the macro- and micro- fauna living within the soil. Harvesting crops removes organic matter which would otherwise be incorporated into the soil. This leads to a reduction in the organic matter content which in turn may affect the water holding capacity and, especially, the structural stability of the soil. Radio-carbon analysis of organic matter from within soils of the English Midlands has given surprisingly old dates of 800 years or more and very little younger material. This suggests the store of organic matter dates from the time of the wildwood. The pasture farming that characterized these areas for most of the past centuries is interpreted as having been of little effect, neither adding to, nor reducing, the organic store. The arable farming of the past 40 years, however, is thought to have had a negative effect causing a progressive reduction in organic matter to the point where soil structures are now beginning to break down and soil erosion is becoming easier and more widespread.

The natural compaction of the soil is modified by the passage of heavy farm machinery, which compresses the soil, thereby decreasing the infiltration capabilities. Since in arable fields machines tend to follow the same tracks, lower-lying runnels with a highly compressed base result. These are natural foci for overland flow and soil erosion if aligned downslope. Much of the recent erosion on the South Downs in Sussex has been concentrated initially in these features (see page 37).

Irrigation of soils is not without its problems especially in semi-arid areas such as southern California and south-east Australia. In these areas, under the artificially wet conditions, salts can migrate to the higher soil horizons and accumulate in toxic quantities. Very careful management is needed to prevent this. Draining soils can also be hazardous, especially in peatlands. Although formed under waterlogged conditions, peat can become irreversibly dried when it is drained (one can moisten only the outside of organic material). If this happens when a dry spell of weather occurs the surface peat dries out and, being exceptionally light, can be subjected to serious wind erosion. Many small drainage ditches rather than a few major ones can prevent this taking place.

The main effects of using the land for farming are to modify or completely change the vegetation thereby altering the water balance of the soil, modifying the natural physical conditions of the soil, and more importantly, at certain times exposing bare soil. This provides the ideal conditions for increasing the speed of erosion above that of the natural rate. It is this aspect of the soil, above all others, that has been affected by human usage. For this reason alone it deserves highlighting again, in spite of the voluminous literature on the topic (Evans and Cook, 1986; Eyles, 1987; Hodges and Arden-Clarke, 1986; Morgan, 1979).

Causes of soil erosion

Erosion of the soil can be an entirely natural phenomenon. In many areas of steep slopes and seasonal, high-intensity rainfall, for example New Zealand, or where steep slopes experience frequent earthquake shocks, as in Papua New Guinea, the natural rate of erosion is relatively high. More important than the actual rate is the fact that under natural conditions the rate of soil loss approximates the rate of soil formation. The limited extent of bare rock indicates this.

Soil erosion, however, is usually understood to imply that the rate of erosion is greater than would occur naturally, that is there is accelerated erosion caused by human interference. Almost any use of the soil for agriculture or modification of the natural vegetation increases the rate of erosion. A small increase may be thought quite acceptable and not a matter of concern. Indeed, there may be almost no signs of the accelerated erosion at this stage. In the long term such a view may be a very complacent one. However, soil erosion usually produces visible signs which alert people to the danger. Rates of soil loss from agricultural land, in the range of 4.5 to 45.0 $kg\,m^{-2}y^{-1}$ almost invariably leave their mark on the landscape. Even so, knowing that soil erosion (accelerated erosion) is taking place or will take place does not necessarily lead to remedial action being taken. This is because curing and preventing erosion involve

both technological and social solutions. Providing the former is usually much easier than organizing the latter.

Erosion of the soil involves the detachment of individual particles or soil aggregates from the soil mass and their transport, largely by water and wind. An important corollary is the deposition that occurs when the energy available for transportation declines.

Stated thus, soil erosion may be thought of as a relatively simple phenomenon. In detail, however, it is very complex since it involves the interaction of the rainfall and windspeeds, soil conditions, vegetation, slope geometry, land use and land management practices, etc., each one of which has a vast range of subtle variations.

Accelerated erosion arises when either the availability of suitable sized particles is increased, or when the power of the transporting mechanism is increased. Human activity can affect both, particularly by changing or modifying the vegetation cover. The natural vegetation may be thought of as a buffer between the climatic elements and the soil. (It may influence climate and soil too.) Vegetation has an important effect upon the eventual end condition of a fall of rain. Most strikingly, the vegetation cover intercepts the raindrops, and by preventing or delaying their journey to the ground enhances evaporation to the extent that total precipitation, as measured above the vegetation, may be reduced in woodlands certainly by 10%, commonly by 20% and occasionally by over 60% (Prandini et al., 1977). This relationship between vegetation and rainfall is very complex. Clearly the amount of rainwater intercepted by lower growing vegetation – shrubs and herbs – will be less than that intercepted by trees since their surface area is smaller, but even with grass the amount is not insubstantial. Leaf size, shape and density are also important, and major contrasts occur between summer and winter in areas of deciduous trees.

The vegetation, however, acts in other ways. Of the rain that does escape being intercepted and evaporated some will re-form and fall as droplets. Except in areas of very tall, long-trunked trees the terminal velocity of these droplets will be lower than that of raindrops impacting directly on the soil. Moving at a slower speed means they possess less energy to erode. But energy to do work also depends on the size of the particle that hits the ground and here, too, the effect of the vegetation is variable. Leaf size and configuration in some species will encourage droplets to be larger than those of the initial rainfall, while other species, particularly conifers, tend to produce secondary droplets that are smaller. Much of the water does not fall as droplets from the vegetation but is channelled towards the trunk or stems of the vegetation and reaches the ground as stem flow. The impact effect of this is negligible although it could contribute to overland flow processes.

Leaf litter on the ground surface acts in similar ways to the growing plants. It intercepts falling droplets and protects the soil against direct impact. It also poses an obstacle to the development of overland flow. Organic material and the abundant and diverse soil fauna it encourages, act separately and together via the humidifying process to enhance the water-absorbing and water-holding capacity of the soil, thereby inhibiting the development of surface run-off. Soil organisms and organic matter also contribute to a good soil structure which makes it more difficult for an individual particle to be detached. The vegetation cover also removes water from the soil via the rooting system and the process of transpiration. This makes available more space within the soil for the next addition of rainwater and so again helps reduce the occurrence of overland flow.

Two other points need to be noted. The first is that vegetation cover reduces the desiccating effects of the Sun and the development of hard crusts on the surface that are impervious to rainwater and hence encourage overland flow. Second, the roots themselves act as an anchor and in the case of many shrubs and trees penetrate sufficiently deeply to reduce the frequency of shallow-sliding types of soil erosion.

It need hardly be stressed, therefore, that soil erosion does not necessarily, or even largely, result from the direct misuse of the soil. Nor does the amount of modification to the vegetation need to be very large. Douglas (1967), working in Peninsula Malaysia in two very similar drainage basins, has shown that in one, with a 94% vegetation cover, the erosion rate is $0.21 \text{ kg m}^{-2}\text{y}^{-1}$ whilst in the other, with a 64% vegetation cover the rate is nearly five times greater at $1.04 \text{ kg m}^{-2}\text{y}^{-1}$.

Many of the influences noted above with reference to water erosion apply also to wind erosion. In particular one should record the influence of the vegetation in reducing the windspeed at the surface. For soil particles of a given size there is a certain minimum windspeed needed before movement will begin. Even an intermittent vegetation cover significantly reduces the windspeed at the ground surface.

Misuse of the soil itself can compound the damage that may be caused by converting land to arable or pastoral use. Essentially, any activity which either increases the proportion of individual particles within the soil (i.e. breaks down soil structures), or which compacts the soil surface and so decreases infiltration, is potentially hazardous. Causes of the former might be failure to replace organic matter within the soil or failure to replace those nutrients removed in harvested crops, since these are both important contributors to the development and maintenance of soil structures. Chemical spraying to kill pests may also kill beneficial organisms (and begs the question of what is a pest). Modern systems of rotivation also tend to break down soil structures as they produce a fine seed bed. Although not at the surface an impervious layer can develop at the base of ploughing where the ploughshare presses onto the soil below. This may become an erosion hazard.

More obvious than these factors is the physical movement of the soil by being ploughed into well-defined ridges and furrows which can act as incipient channels if angled downslope.

Types of soil erosion

Soil erosion takes the form of a number of well-defined types that have been recognized for almost as long as the soil has been cultivated. Several well-known texts deal with this topic with clarity and in some detail (Morgan, 1979). Here only the barest outline of the main types will be given.

Rainsplash erosion

On bare soil on sloping terrain rainsplash erosion may be an important, if not spectacular, cause of erosion. It is of considerable potency in areas of high-intensity rainfall, especially where this coincides with a large raindrop size as it often does in the tropics. The process is, perhaps, most easily understood by considering the fate of a single raindrop. Falling unimpeded from a great height it arrives at the ground surface at its terminal velocity, duly modified by the effects of size, windspeed and direction in relation to the slope, and possessing kinetic energy with which to do work or erosion. Most of this energy is dissipated in friction as the droplet moves across or into the surface (only 0.2% of the energy of a falling raindrop is available for erosion (Rubey, 1952; Pearce, 1976)). The action of the raindrop at the soil surface is twofold. First, it acts like a miniature battering ram, compacting the soil surface. This produces a thin soil crust which may hinder the penetration into the soil of subsequent droplets and thereby encourage overland flow. Second, it causes some soil particles to move, launching them into the air. On flat ground they will fall back around the impact point, but on sloping land those moving downslope will necessarily move further than those moving back up the slope. These particles, in turn, transfer their own momentum onto other particles which themselves move if the kinetic energy exceeds the frictional forces keeping them in position. The outcome of this process being repeated by all the raindrops falling on the slope is to cause a net downslope transfer of material.

This brief outline necessarily hides many minor but significant features which make predicting the results of rainsplash erosion an exacting task. Variation in impact velocity, droplet size and droplet shape usually vary temporally and spatially in a rainstorm. The effects vary with slope angle. They are greatly influenced by the textural and structural characteristics of the soil, and by the amount of moisture already present. Thus, a droplet impacting on a dry soil has a different quantitative effect from one landing on a wet soil because of contrasts in the cohesiveness of the soils, and this, in turn, differs from one landing in a thin layer of water which absorbs most of the raindrop's energy.

Because rainsplash acts uniformly over the surface, and usually involves only small movements, its visual effects are often very subtle. One piece of field evidence for its occurrence is the existence of splash pedestals or soil pillars. Morgan (1977) records pedestals 2 cm high forming in one year on sandy soils in Bedfordshire. The build up of soil on the upslope side of a hedge is another sign.

Sheet erosion or soil wash

If a rainstorm is heavy enough, or of long enough duration, the capacity of the soil to absorb further additions of water is exceeded. In such circumstances water begins to flow across the surface as overland flow. Several types of erosion relating to overland flow have been recognized, of which sheet erosion is, arguably, one of the least common. At its simplest (and rarest) one has a thin sheet of turbulent water moving downslope at a speed sufficient to cause previously static soil particles to move. As with rainsplash erosion a large range of variables interact during the process and so help explain why apparently similar conditions may produce quite different results. For example, erosion will vary according to the particle size and textural mix of the soil.

Rill erosion

In practice conditions rarely exist enabling a uniform sheet of water to flow across the ground surface. Usually the flow is broken up by stones and plants and by surface irregularities. The result is the formation of a myriad of micro-channels that are constantly altering their position as they become blocked by debris or 'captured' by adjacent channels. Typically, they are V-shaped in cross-section, although in sandy soils they may be more rectangular. They may be several centimetres deep, they are usually spaced at intervals varying from a metre or less to tens of metres, but they can be quite isolated. They tend to be discontinuous in the sense of petering out before reaching a stream. In fact the term channel is too strong a word to describe these features which are markedly ephemeral. The net effect of the process is to produce a relatively uniform loss of soil across the whole slope. At the end of a rainstorm minor channels may exist, but these are quickly eliminated by the action of the soil fauna, further lighter rain, wind and frost. When they re-form, a new network occurs unrelated to the position of the previous channels. Rilling is a potent process in semi-arid areas where high intensity rainstorms are quite characteristic. One classic study is that by Schumm (1956) in the badlands near South Dakota in the USA.

Rilling is not unknown in Britain. Indeed, it seems to be becoming more common and has been reported over recent years from several areas, including Bedfordshire (Morgan, 1977) and the South Downs near Brighton (Robinson and Williams, 1988; Robinson and Blackman, 1989). Estimates suggest that soil losses in the latter area totalled in excess of 200 tonnes per hectare from one major storm and other smaller events in October 1987. This is equivalent to losing 2cm of topsoil across a whole field. Since downland soils are relatively thin (30 cm or less) sustained losses of this order have serious implications for agriculture (fig. 7).

As is so often the case, the event-triggering storm on the South Downs in October 1987 was not a particularly severe one. A nearby rain-gauge recorded 67 mm of rain, a figure that has been exceeded before. There is no evidence to suggest that storms are now more frequent. Hence, one must look for additional factors when trying to explain the increased erosion over the past two decades. A change in land use from pastureland to arable is a basic factor but, more important would seem to be the change from sowing spring cereal crops to autumn sown varieties. This exposes the soil to heavier and more effective rainfall, and because growth is slow, exposes it for a longer period of time. It is also suggested that a reduced organic content in the soil, due to the less frequent use of grass leys in the system of rotation, has led to a weakened soil structure, while the removal of hedges and the consequent enlarged field size has reduced the number of checks to the water as it flows downhill. The fine tilth that is now produced by modern machinery may also be a factor, as are the ruts produced by tractor wheels which provide ready-made channel ways.

Gully erosion

Just as rills can form a continuum with surface wash, so larger, master rills may develop to the extent that they become permanent features of the land surface and evolve into gullies. Gullies may, however, develop directly from overland flow. They are not, therefore, simply overgrown rills, even though they are often associated with them and with the same environmental conditions.

Gullies are steep-sided, permanent channel ways which experience ephemeral flow during rainstorms. V-shaped cross-sections are characteristic but steep-sided, flat-floored gullies, for example on the volcanic plateau of New Zealand (Blong, 1966, 1970) have been reported from too many areas to be regarded as exceptional. They have an immense size range. Smaller ones may be 2 m deep and 1 m across at the top, and extend tens of metres in length. Larger gullies may exceed 20 m in depth, 20–30 m in width and

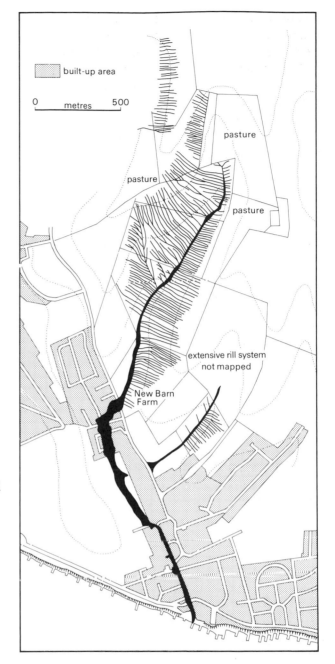

Figure 7   **Rill system developed on the South Downs, near Rottingdean, in 1987.**
Source: Robinson and Williams (1988)

extend for over a kilometre. Several gullies may form within a single field but equally they may be quite isolated features with less than a dozen occurring within ten square kilometres.

As noted above some gullies develop from a master rill, a situation that seems to have occurred in the South Downs. Others, however, develop by headward retreat, having originated at some break of slope on the hillside or valley bottom. This type of gully, which is highly characteristic of the volcanic pumice lands of New Zealand (Blong, 1970), heads backwards when overland flow falls over the lip previously created, and undercuts the

Plate 6 *Gully on the Mid Dorme, Soil Conservation Reserve, Southland, New Zealand, before treatment. The poor vegetation cover and secondary rilling on the gully sides are evident. Overstocking was the prime cause of this gully. Stock removal, oversowing with grasses and clovers, top-dressing with fertilizers and a tree planting programme have repaired much of the damage over the past 20 years.*
Photo: NZ Dept. of Conservation

base of the head-wall, which then collapses, causing further retreat. The rate of back cutting can be dramatic. One gully is known to have extended back over several hundred metres in one winter (Blong, 1966).

Other gullies form as a result of the collapse of natural pipes and tunnels. They are especially common in areas of loessic soils, having been described from as far afield as the USA (Buckham and Cockfield, 1950), Hungary and New Zealand, where, on the Wither Hills near Blenheim, they have proved a major headache for soil conservators for many years (Laffen *et al.*, 1977).

Mass movement – slip erosion

In semi-arid areas with a sparse vegetation cover, and in areas of arable farming, much of the soil erosion is of the wash–rill–gully type. In areas of farming based on European pastures, the mat type of cover largely precludes wash and rilling, although gully erosion can occur, as illustrated in New Zealand. However, given a good, but not natural vegetation cover, soil erosion can be a serious problem through the action of 'slip' erosion (more generally termed landsliding). This is especially prevalent in areas where high-total and high-intensity rainfall are associated with moderate to high temperatures and steep slopes (plate 7).

New Zealand has the doubtful privilege of affording many examples of this type of soil erosion (fig. 8). The warm, moist conditions are important in encouraging the continued chemical weathering of the regolith. A clay-rich parent material may also create the same conditions. This leads towards the creation of soils rich in clay minerals. Soils of this type usually respond to periods of wetting and drying by expanding and contracting as they gain or lose moisture. Cracks often develop which act as near-vertical lines of weakness in the soil mass. There is, too, quite often a sharp demarcation between the soil and the weathered bedrock which may act as a lateral line of weakness.

In fact, the continuous root mat in the upper soil layers is often the major control holding the soil together. In a heavy rainstorm these clay-rich soils absorb water and hence have their weight increased. At the same time the weak bonds holding the clay particles together are forced apart as the pressure inside the pore spaces is increased. As a result, the balance between the forces holding the soil together and these forces acting to push it apart, narrows. Once a certain critical level is exceeded slope failure may take place. A good example of this type of soil erosion is provided by the storms of 1977 which affected the Wairarapa area of New Zealand (Crozier *et al.*, 1980).

Plate 7 *A now classic photograph taken on the Napier to Wairoa highway, Hawkes Bay, New Zealand, in 1938 following a very severe storm. Although the intensity and quantity of the rainfall was the major factor inducing such widespread slip erosion, clearing the land of forest was the key contributory factor. Less than optimal pasture management only exacerbated the problem. Such slips, although rarely as devastating as in this photograph, are still common following exceptionally heavy or long-continued rainstorms.*
Photo: NZ Dept. of Conservation

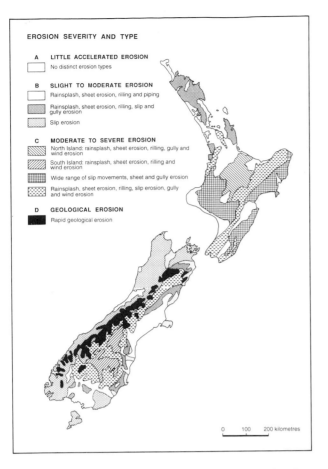

Figure 8   The degree and type of soil erosion in New Zealand.
Source: Howard, 1970

Soil erosion of this form is less common in cool temperate areas, but is occasionally recorded. In Britain the Exmoor storm of 1952 led to quite severe erosion of this type (Gifford, 1953).

Wind erosion

The dust storms that formed such a feature of Oklahoma and Kansas in the 1920s and 1930s, and which are regularly reported from various parts of the world every day (Saharan dust lands in Britain!), are the most dramatic indicators of soil erosion by wind. Less obvious wind erosion occurs in many areas, as householders in East Anglia can testify, as they sweep up dust inside and wash down exterior paintwork.

Almost by definition wind erosion is most effective in areas where bare soils occur, either because of sparse, often modified vegetation or through arable farming. Many of the world's rangelands are susceptible to this type of damage. The dry lands of sub-Saharan Africa provide extensive examples. Wind erosion of arable land has been reported in recent years from Khazakstan, from Australia and from New Zealand's South Island, as well as from Britain.

In common with the other soil-eroding processes discussed, the details of wind erosion are extremely complex. Soil condition, particle size, surface roughness and windspeed are merely four of many interactive variables. Essentially, however, soil particles are lifted up by the application of a sufficiently large fluid force (wind) and movement is further enhanced by the bombardment of the soil by grains already in motion. Clearly, therefore, any land use practice which increases the area of bare soil and/or leads to the breakdown of the soil to its smallest constituents, reducing soil structures, is potentially damaging. In this connection the loss of organic matter from the soil is particularly serious and much of the recent wind losses in the heavy clay soils of England's East Midlands have been attributable to this, although modern techniques which produce a finer tilth may also have contributed to the problem.

Remedial measures

It has been shown that although in itself soil erosion is a fairly simple phenomenon, in detail its physical causes are extremely complex and the degree and consequences of erosion variable. The response to soil erosion is also variable. At one level a change in land use practice is all that is required; at another level engineering works may be needed. This is examined in the case study of the Whareama catchment, New Zealand, on pages 40 and 41. However, economic, social and political factors all interact to make the human response to soil erosion uncertain (Blaikie, 1985).

Soil erosion may range from being just a little faster than the natural erosion rate to being so fast that visible damage can be seen. Perhaps the individual farmers and nations can live with the former; almost certainly they cannot, or should not, live with the latter. Any remedial action must involve increased expenses, at least in the short term, although long term it may be profitable. The ability to pay the short-term charges will be almost infinitely variable. Two adjacent freehold farms do not necessarily have similar financial positions. One may be a long-established family farm, the other might be under new ownership and be

Case study: the Whareama story – Wairarapa, New Zealand

The Whareama Catchment Control Scheme was the first of its kind in New Zealand. It arose partly because of the increasing frequency and intensity of flooding, particularly in the settlement of Tinui, and partly because of the severe hill country erosion associated with the floods. The origins of the story can be traced back to the 1850s when the area was first opened up to farming; a new chapter opened in 1956 with the beginnings of a comprehensive conservation programme; the story continues with a sustained management programme into the 1990s (WASCO, 1987).

Physical background
The Whareama catchment is predominately hilly. Stream density is high and the relative relief often exceeds 250–300 m. Slopes, therefore, are steep, often in excess of 20°, and long. The underlying geology comprises deeply weathered sandstones and argillites or mudstones. Much of the area is shattered by faulting, giving crush zones. The climate of the area comprises warm, generally dry summers, and cooler, much wetter winters. Rainfall, the key to the erosion and flooding, exceeds 1000 mm in the lowlands and increases to more than 1300 mm in the higher areas. Significantly, much of it falls in high-intensity rainstorms. This combination of physical conditions is highly conducive to erosion.

History
The first sheep were pastured in the area about 1844. There followed a period of pastoral expansion with the establishment of, by British standards, very large farms (often in excess of 5000 ha). Many of these have since been sub-divided. This was accompanied by clearing the hills of the natural vegetation – mainly scrub and fern but with some forest – and draining the river flats. In a very short period this greatly increased what had been already a very high rate of natural erosion. Erosion was exacerbated by the introduction and spread of rabbits after 1880, this problem being contained only after 1950. Clearing the land decreased slope stability and also increased surface run-off. This led to erosion of both the hill-slopes and the stream banks. In an attempt to stabilize the banks, crack willows were planted by the early settlers. These grew vigorously and spread rapidly as branches, broken off in floods, rooted themselves. As a result the river channels became choked and unable to remove the flood water; hence flooding became a problem. In the 1890s attempts were made to clear the willows but in the process many twigs and branches fell into the streams and acted as new growth points, thus compounding the problem. Conditions generally deteriorated and were not helped by the Great Depression of the 1930s and the two World Wars.

The crisis point was reached in 1956 when three large floods inundated the valley flats and caused extensive erosion. A call was made for a comprehensive plan to deal with the problem. The Wairarapa Catchment Board was approached and, after initial pilot surveys, a minute study of the whole catchment was undertaken, the outcome of which was a detailed proposal for a catchment control scheme for the Whareama, to be financed two-thirds from central government and one-third from a special district rate. Additionally farm plans were drawn up to counter specific soil erosion problems to which the individual farmer would contribute one-third of the costs.

The problems
By 1956, therefore, the problems facing the area were flooding due to willow choking, and soil erosion. This latter took the form of shallow slips and earthflow, gully erosion, slumping (massive, deep earth movements on relatively low angled slopes), and bank erosion.

The remedies
Commencing in 1957 a programme of willow eradication was initiated to control flooding. All willows were cut into short lengths. The stumps were painted with the anti-growth hormone 2,4-D and the trash allowed to wash down river into the sea. The following season any regrowth was again dosed in 2,4-D. By 1967 the Whareama was cleared back to Tinui and three major tributaries had also been dealt with. Bank erosion, caused mainly by vigorous channel downcutting, was combatted by constructing small debris dams across the streams to trap the silt. These might be built every 20 metres or so depending on the slope

of the stream. Correspondingly larger structures (trestle dams) were erected where the valley floor opened out. Where bank erosion was the result of undercutting, the bank was protected by wire netting and railings arranged so as to deflect the main flow away from the vulnerable bank. On suitable sites in small catchments, regulating earth dams were built to impound flood water and release a controlled flow into the gully system.

Gully head erosion has proved difficult to overcome but some success has been achieved by grading the headwall and covering it (thatching) with scrub and wire netting, often arranged in a series of gentle drops.

Slope erosion is caused by too much water. To combat this, seepage points, often the site of major slumps, are drained and flows piped to safe outlets. More generally, excess slope water is removed by planting trees which draw water up through their roots and transpire it. Species compatible with grassland farming have been planted, notably Italian hybrid poplars and the willow *Salix matsudana*. Open tree planting is the largest single erosion control requirement in the catchment. However, the importance of the remaining native vegetation is recognized and efforts have been made to encourage vigorous growth by fencing it off from grazing animals. Sometimes very severe erosion necessitated the complete retirement of land from grazing and its close planting with seedling trees.

All this was accompanied by the adoption of sound grassland management practices, utilizing fertilizers, optimum stocking rates, etc.

The results
Within 10 years of the scheme starting, flood levels had been reduced by as much as 5 m for a given rainfall and the incidence of floods in the settlement of Tinui greatly reduced. Soil erosion is

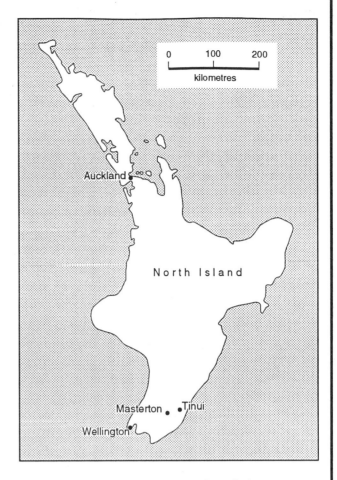

North Island, New Zealand: location of places mentioned in the text.

much reduced and the land-carrying capacity consequently has increased. Some farms have doubled the number of sheep they can run. One estimate suggests that every New Zealand dollar spent on the scheme has generated four and a half extra dollars. No less important has been the increased confidence that the scheme has brought to the area. Nevertheless, the underlying physical conditions of the area – its geology, climate, relief and soil – remain. Hence adherence to sound land management practices and conservation techniques remains an ongoing requirement.

burdened by a huge mortgage. Alternatively, adjacent farms may differ greatly in size and the smaller of the two might now be only marginally profitable because of changed economic conditions. In these circumstances any new incurred debt might never be repaid. Again, a freehold farmer might view his or her land in a different light to that of a tenant farmer, or an absentee landowner. External financial assistance in one country might be vastly more generous than in another. Finally, access to advice and the quality of advice will vary, not only from country to country, but even from region to region. Numerous other factors also operate to make the adoption of soil conservation measures a complex matter.

The actual occurrence of soil erosion is the result of physical factors. The events leading up to the condition are mainly social and economic. Ignorance of good farming practice is one factor; simple greed, the desire to make the biggest profits in the shortest time irrespective of the consequences, is another; a calculated judgement on medium-term management plans that proves wrong is a third. Even conservative land use practice may be overwhelmed by an exceptional, once in 500 years, rainstorm. Many of the problems arise, not directly because of wilful, bad farming, but because the economic conditions within which farmers operate virtually dictate that bad, or at least less than optimum, farming practices are the only ones that can reasonably be expected. In this connection the land-holding system may be at fault, or the price farmers obtain for their produce may be kept artificially low by a central government following a cheap food policy. The price of fertilizers, machinery and good stock may be too high. Farmers may get inadequate or insufficient advice from government agencies. One might even argue that by failing to spend enough money on rural schooling generally, some countries create a situation in which farmers may lack the educational competence to cope with all but the simplest modern techniques, or to appraise new ideas.

One must note, however, that soil erosion may not be the result of inappropriate farming. It can be caused by the general population seeking firewood and destroying the vegetation; it may result from forestry activities; it can even result from the pressure of tourism and the tramp of feet, as happened on Ilkley Moor, West Yorkshire, UK, for example.

There are remedial methods available. It should be noted, however, that the pace of soil formation is slow and that it is difficult to speed it up. Thus conservation techniques need to be ongoing. Destruction is almost always easier than reconstruction.

Soil erosion may be tackled in various ways according to the nature, extent and degree of erosion (Hudson, 1981; Morgan, 1979). It may be necessary to take a whole catchment approach if climate, relief and geology have combined to produce uniformly severe erosion over a very large area. In these circumstances an important step is to classify the land within the area according to its capability to sustain a particular land use and then to recommend (or even order) a land use plan for the area (WSDNZ, 1969; Dent and Young, 1981).

Several such land capability schemes exist, the basis of them all being that as the physical conditions deteriorate, limits are set upon the types and range of land use that can be sustained without damage to the environment. Thus Class I land has few limits for any type of farming and can be used safely for highly intensive activities although, of course, it could be used for extensive farming or even for forestry or simply leisure purposes. Whether the last course of action makes economic or social sense depends on other circumstances. In contrast Class VIII land has many limitations for agriculture and forestry and should be left unused except, perhaps, for recreational hunting, controlled leisure activities or as a biological reserve.

Once the land within a catchment has been classified in this way an appropriate land use pattern can be established. In catchments susceptible to erosion this often means limiting cropping to a few specific crops on the valley-bottom lands, restricting extensive sheep or cattle grazing within well-defined areas, and leaving significant steepland and upland areas to either plantation forestry or areas of natural vegetation.

It is quite possible that soil erosion is a problem specific to one farm, and one farmer may seek advice for his or her specific problems. In this case a whole-farm approach may be adopted. A land capability assessment again forms the basis of any plan, but in this case more local detail is added. This may involve the resiting of fence-lines to discourage stock gathering at vulnerable locations, or even the establishment of fences to enable stock to be monitored and moved more easily (McCaskill, 1973). On arable farms it could mean adopting a different rotation pattern or establishing simple soil conservation techniques.

In areas where soil conservation techniques can be shown to be advantageous but do not justify substantial expense, a simple ridge and furrow system may be adopted. This is achieved by tilling the ground into 10 m wide parallel ridges with intervening furrows about half a metre deep and a gradient of 1:400. An even simpler remedy is to plough along the contours, thereby avoiding furrows and depressions running downslope and encouraging run-off to concentrate and cause scour erosion. Contoured strip cropping, using a repeated downslope sequence of two or three crops with differing planting and harvesting times, perhaps linked with grass strips, is another well-used technique.

By using different crops harvesting and tillage periods can be varied so that at any one time exposed soil is limited, thereby minimizing the risk of erosion. Protection can be enhanced with sound tillage practices such as leaving a large percentage of residual material (leaves, stalks, crowns and roots) on or near the surface as a protective mulch. A bare loose surface can also be avoided by using herbicides to control weeds instead of tillage. Strip cropping and contour ploughing may also be the preferred means of tackling a specific area of soil erosion on one farm. Another common technique, which uses one of the simplest structures involved in soil conservation, is the storm-water drain (or diversion ditch). This is a ditch, or open drain, which intercepts and diverts water which would otherwise flow down onto arable land from higher ground. It is rarely found on its own. It is usually an integral part of an inter-linked protection system. It is essentially the first line of defence and is designed to prevent uncontrolled water reaching arable land from outside. All other structures in the scheme will be designed on this assumption.

Within an arable area channel terraces (bunds) may be constructed at right angles to the steepest slope to prevent surface run-off building up to the point where it can commence scour action. They comprise an excavated channel with a bank on the downhill side formed from the spoil from the excavation. Some are designed with a slight gradient for the purpose of removing surplus water off the arable land at non-erosive velocities.

Others are truly horizontal, any water collecting on them infiltrating into the soil. They may or may not have closed ends.

Water from storm-water drains and graded channel terraces is discharged either into a natural water course or, where one does not exist, into artificial waterways. The latter have a bank on each side to contain the water and are generally grassed over, hence the name grass or sod waterways or meadow strips. Although the concept is relatively simple the precise design features such as width, slope, bank height, channel depth and spacing are not unimportant since they determine the effectiveness of the structure, the amount of land lost to production and access across the slope.

The channel terrace and its variants is fundamentally different from the bench terrace, which is often used on very steep slopes to create level areas of ground capable of cultivation and almost incidentally aids soil conservation. A hill-slope modified by bench terracing comprises a series of horizontal, or nearly horizontal, treads (benches or ledges), and vertical, or near vertical, risers. To hold up the vertical face some structural wall is needed, usually of stone, but sometimes of brick or timber (Hudson, 1981).

The labour needed to construct bench terraces is enormous, hence they are rarely built today – indeed many have fallen into a state of disrepair. Even so they are widespread, transcultural features occurring in such diverse areas as Peru (Machu Picchu), Nepal, Indonesia, China and Japan, the Phillipines, the Mediterranean area and the Rhine gorge in Germany.

Bench terraces may be constructed on a contour to minimize run-off, or with a slight gradient. However, on these steep slopes channelling run-off down the slope without causing gullying is not easy. The tread itself may be flat, sloping slightly outward, or slightly inward. In all cases where cropping is practical the wider the tread the better.

The special demands of growing rice on terraced land requires a raised lip at the outer edge of the tread and a level surface in order to retain the water. When properly maintained the effectiveness of terracing as a conservation technique is shown by the antiquity of many functioning examples.

Alternatively, for practical reasons, it may only be

possible to tackle directly the immediate problem. In some cases this may mean resting the land for up to five, or even ten years. Such a scheme was initiated with some success in the Mba area of Fiji in the mid-1960s following extensive and severe erosion caused by firing and overgrazing (Cochrane, 1969; Liedke, 1989). Clearly though, the capability of a farm to sustain the withdrawal of part of its land from production, however small that might be, is variable. The loss of, say, 200 ha on a large farm might be relatively unimportant whereas on a smaller farm such a loss may provoke severe economic strain.

To speed up the rehabilitation process, oversowing with grasses and clovers appropriate to the soils of the area, plus fertilizing, may be desirable. This, too, is a cost which has to be borne by the farmer.

In cases of severe gully erosion various engineering solutions may have to be adopted. These can range from the construction of dams (quite simple ones) along the gully, to the bulldozing and infilling of the gully. Quick-growing, ground-covering plants usually accompany this approach. An engineering solution may be appropriate in less severe cases too and, indeed, as a preventive measure. The remoulding of the slope into a series of terraces is one solution. Various types are used (see Morgan, 1979 for a summary) depending on the precise climatic, soil and slope conditions but each has the objective of shortening slope length and reducing the slope angle thereby inhibiting overland flow.

As with surface water erosion, wind erosion is less effective if there is a ground vegetation cover. Conservation practices in this context generally aim to produce either a crop mix which minimizes the area of bare ground at any one time, combined with a tillage regime that disturbs the surface as little as possible, or a stocking regime which prevents overgrazing. The planting of shelter belts to reduce the windspeed is an old-established practice, but as the size of machinery has increased and the need for larger fields developed, their effectiveness has diminished, although their importance remains (Sturroch, 1981).

Erosion and conservation in Britain

The nature and types of soil erosion and soil conser-vation have been well documented by many writers including Bennett (1939) Hudson (1971) and Morgan (1979). They have been included here in some detail because so much of the farmed areas of the world still experiences important soil losses in spite of well-established strategies for erosion control (Hudson, 1971).

The topic has assumed greater prominence in Britain in recent years as reports of rilling and gullying appear to have become more frequent (Boardman et al., 1990), and research into the problem has expanded (Morgan, 1977). The effects of rilling on fields in the South Downs has already been mentioned (Boardman et al., 1990; Robinson and Boardman, 1988; Boardman and Robinson, 1985), but it has been reported from many other localities, either in professional publications or the local press. Among the former a nationwide survey has been made by Evans and Cook (1986) and Evans (1988), while localised examples are provided by Colborne and Staines (1985) for Somerset, Evans and Northcliffe (1978) in Norfolk, Morgan et al. (1987) in Bedfordshire, and by Ternan (1979–82) in the Tamar valley in south-west England. Personal observations have shown that rill erosion occurred in south-east Hertfordshire in 1988.

Qualitative reports of a broadly similar nature have been made in the past, for example White (1851) and Oakley (1945), but one is left with the impression that in the 15 years to 1990 rilling has become more commonplace. Certainly, recent developments in land use practices have produced conditions that might encourage erosion. Among these are the production of extremely fine, even seed beds (the better to apply herbicides), the trend towards autumn sowing of cereals, and the repeated use of tractor lines during successive crop management operations. Fine, even seed beds ease the development of surface water movement. Autumn planting exposes the ground to potential rain attack for a longer period at the time of year characterized by periods of heavy rainfall. Tractor lines provide ready-made channels for overland flow to exploit.

Erosion, however, is not limited to, or even most widespread on, cereal fields. Market-garden crops such as potatoes and carrots are especially vulnerable given the nature of the ground preparation and the length of time the soil is bare, or almost bare, of cover with these crops (Agassi et al., 1989). For these crops spring is the main period of erosion danger.

In all cases lack of vegetation cover is a key factor encouraging erosion. Studies suggest that erosion is a potential hazard while the ground cover is less than about 10% (Robinson and Boardman, 1988), although it has been reported in fields with a 25% to 30% cover (Stocking, 1976; Evans, 1990).

The type of soil onto which the rain falls is a second factor affecting erosion. There is considerable evidence to suggest that light textured, and especially sandy soils, are particularly susceptible to rilling (Evans, 1980; Reed, 1979). In contrast to this the influence of slope morphology is not entirely clear. Data collected by Evans (1988) appears to show that rilling tends to occur on slopes exceeding 3°, but only where a long (> 50 m) upslope convexity occurs.

A further variable related to the erosion problem is the actual rainfall needed to initiate movement. In essence erosion may be observed either after short-duration, high-intensity storms, or after lower-intensity but longer-duration periods of rainfall. The amount of water present in the soil prior to the rainfall is also important. Significantly, only a few studies have been able to link observed erosion with near, or on-site rainfall records (Morgan, 1977; Saull, 1983), but these indicate that rains were often less than 25 mm in amount, and intensities were less than 3 mm per hour. These cannot be considered uncommon events.

In countries such as the USA and New Zealand soil conservation practices have a high profile (McCaskill, 1973), yet they are little used in Britain at present in spite of the fact that techniques of erosion control are well established and widely known.

As outlined earlier the basic initial step in any conservation programme is to undertake a land capability assessment. With this information a conservation scheme can be drawn up using agronomic techniques, mechanical measures and/or soil management practices as appropriate.

However, this information needs to be set within an economic context. One needs to ask how much erosion is costing now, and is likely to cost in the future in lost production, and set this against the costs of a conservation programme and the benefits this might bring.

Until the benefits exceed the costs there can be, at best, only slow progress. At present in Britain the economic impact of soil erosion remains largely unstudied (Boardman, 1989), and this, taken in conjunction with the less than dramatic nature of soil erosion, means that the implementation of even low-cost conservation methods is uncommon.

4 The land: scratching the surface

Introduction

The previous chapters have emphasized the importance of climate, soil and vegetation for the successful functioning of this planet, highlighted their value as resources and stressed the ease with which they can be modified, often deleteriously. The land surface and near-land surface are no less important. Above all else human beings are surface dwellers. A few still resort to caves for temporary shelter in the same way as the dreamtime aboriginals of Australia, and the Palaeolithic hunters of Europe who drew the cave pictures at Lascaux in south-west France. Today, however, shelter, when needed, is usually provided by artificial structures (of varying complexity). A small number of us work underground, sail the oceans, or fly, but basically we are creatures of the land surface.

The shape of the Earth's surface has had a major impact upon human organization and activity from the very earliest times. History is full of examples of sites defended in part by their topography. These include the Iron Age hill forts found in many areas of Britain and the location of Hadrian's Wall, the sites of the 12th-century Catharic castles of Peyrepertuse, Queribus and Puilaurens near Perpignan in south-eastern France, the hill-top villages of Mediterranean France and Italy, and the Maori pas which are such a feature of the Waikato, Auckland and Northland areas of New Zealand. Changing technologies have rendered many of these sites historic curios now, but others, by changing their function, have survived as the nucleus of a modern settlement, often attaining the status of tourist sites.

In times of war the shape of the land has often had a profound influence on both defensive and offensive strategies. The Gate of Carcassonne in southern France, a natural routeway overlooked by the Montagne Noire to the north and the limestone hills of Corbières to the south, was one such feature of importance in medieval times; the Vimy Ridge, Paschendaele, the Somme Valley and others achieved notoriety during the First World War (Rosenbaum, 1989), while Mt Harriet was a significant feature of the Falklands War of 1982.

Commercial lines of communication are similarly strongly influenced by the shape of the land, and so is the siting of many towns and settlements. Prehistoric routeways like the Icknield Way, which follows the drier chalk ridge of the Chiltern Hills for part of its length, provide examples, no less than the canals and railways of the Industrial Revolution. Even modern roadbuilding is not entirely free of topographic considerations, particularly in hilly or mountainous areas, as the astonishing Karakorum highway in northern Pakistan demonstrates (Jones et al., 1983). Topographic influences are also relevant to the siting of a modern airport as the debate in the 1960s and 1970s about alternative sites for London's third airport showed.

The shape of the land may also impose opportunities and restraints upon towns and cities, although it is rarely the only, or even the major, factor involved in limiting or encouraging growth. Indeed several world cities such as Hong Kong, Los Angeles and Rio de Janeiro have, at huge cost, seemingly overcome topographic problems and turned them to their advantage. On the other hand the topographic constraints imposed by the hills within and around Wellington, New Zealand, must be one factor that has prevented this capital city growing as rapidly as Auckland, its northern neighbour.

The influence of the shape of the land surface upon human activities is not restricted to urban environments. Slope geometry is an important control of soil erosion and, thus, can play a significant role in rural land use systems and in land management practices. More recently, with increasing affluence and leisure time, the value of the shape of the land as scenery has come to be recognized (Cooke and Doornkamp, 1974; Buckland, 1988). This has found expression in Britain in the establishment of National Parks and Areas of Outstanding Natural Beauty.

Human response to the varied opportunities and costs afforded by the surface and near-surface has been varied. Deliberate attempts have been made to increase the land area, mainly through reclamation. Slope angles have been modified to enable building and farming to expand onto hitherto unsuitable slopes. In many areas hazard mitigation systems have been developed to enable potentially dangerous areas to be utilized. This has been particularly true in volcanic and tectonically unstable zones.

Occasionally human action has reduced the land area available for human use through contamination. The Maralinga area of South Australia, made radioactive by testing atomic bombs in the 1950s, is one such area; Mururoa Atoll in French Polynesia is another. The immediate hinterland of the Chernobyl nuclear power plant in the Ukraine is a more recent zone of exclusion.

The shape of the surface has also been affected by mining and quarrying. These activities have created new slopes through excavation, subsidence and the tipping of waste material. Indeed it is in this context that some of the biggest changes to the surface configuration have been made.

Unlike natural processes, human modification of the Earth's surface has been determined largely by economic forces although in places burial mounds and fortifications indicate that religious and military influences have been strong. The human capacity to alter the surface form has been increased as technology has developed so that today change can be both quicker and on a larger scale than ever before. Human activity can be largely independent of climate and, uniquely, can be very precise in terms of location. In spite of all this activity actual changes to the shape of the land surface have been small relative to the scale of the natural topography. Nevertheless, the changes have been unquestionably very extensive.

The importance of human action on the physical environment is examined in many texts and articles. The classic study *Man and Nature; or Physical Geography as modified by Human Action*, by G. P. Marsh (1864), and the influential *Man as a Geological Agent* by R. L. Sherlock (1922) are two early products of this genre. More recent books such as these by Goudie (1981) and Cooke and Doornkamp (1990) develop this theme. Growing concern with the environment at international, governmental and local levels has been one of the factors that has stimulated geomorphological research into the interaction between human activities and the environment.

The resulting output over the past twenty years has been impressive (Cooke and Doornkamp, 1990) and the contribution of geomorphologists to environmental management has been significant.

Land reclamation

Both lake margin and coastal sites have figured in land reclamation schemes. Until recently such schemes have tended to be applauded as signs of human ingenuity and technical ability. More recently their damage to ecologically important wetland sites has been highlighted. One such example was the outcry in the 1970s by conservationists over plans to reclaim land at Foulness, Essex, for a new airport serving London. At the end of the 1980s the focus had shifted to the Rainham Marshes, also in Essex, and the proposals to construct a vast leisure centre. Further afield, plans to reclaim 1700 ha of Lake Wairarapa, near Wellington, New Zealand, to produce high-quality, low-lying farmland aroused much local opposition and were eventually abandoned (MacLean, 1982). Yet many examples of completed schemes exist, particularly in western Europe where natural conditions and economic and social forces have reinforced each other. Two areas provide outstanding examples: the fenlands in Britain and the polderlands of the Netherlands. In the former, nearly 50,000 ha of land have been added, in the latter over 800,000 ha. In both cases early schemes were directed more at giving protection from sea flooding to land already farmed than to reclaiming the sea bed.

With sea level rising almost continuously in historic times over much of the North Sea Basin, protection against the sea appears to have been the objective of the sea walls built by the Romans in the 1st century AD along portions of the Wash. It was also the driving force for the earliest schemes in the Netherlands. Once the sea was excluded, fenny and swampy areas previously unfarmed could be drained and brought into production. The draining of the Haarlemmermeer south-west of Amsterdam in the mid-19th century is one example, the still incomplete draining of the Ijsselmeer is another (fig. 9).

The cost of protecting and reclaiming land is high but the cost of creating new land by extending the land through filling and dumping is even greater. For this reason land creation schemes tend to be

48

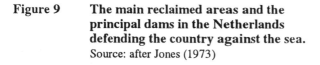

Dam

1 Afsluitdijk Dam
2 Hollandse Ijssel
3 Zandkreek Dam
4 Veerse Gat Dam
5 Grevelingen Dam
6 Volkerak Dam
7 Haringvliet Dam
8 Brouwers Dam
9 Eastern Scheldt Dam
10 Philips Dam
11 Oysterdam

Land drained and
reclaimed from the sea

North Sea

Netherlands

Ijsselmeer

Amsterdam

Rotterdam

Lek River

Waal River

Germany

Maas River

Lower Rhine River

Belgium

0   50   100
kilometres

Figure 9   **The main reclaimed areas and the principal dams in the Netherlands defending the country against the sea.**
Source: after Jones (1973)

restricted to extending land in urban areas, and are generally less ambitious in scale. Many of these schemes have been associated with port facilities, extending the land area seawards to enable ships to berth in deep waters. This is well illustrated by the port at Wellington, New Zealand, where the original 1840 shoreline of the European settlement period is now, in places, over 200 m from the waterfront, and marked only by brass heritage signs (fig. 10). Land extension by filling and dumping has also taken place to extend the runway at Rongatai airport, Wellington, as it has in Hong Kong for the Kai Tak airport. Hong Kong, along with Tokyo, also provides major examples of land extension for commercial building purposes. In both cases a major driving force for this vastly expensive operation has been the shortage of land suitable for building purposes.

In contrast to the planned schemes designed to extend the land area there are many instances at the coast where human activity appears to have contributed to increasing erosion rates and, hence, helped reduce the land area. The erosion of sand dunes (a natural extension of the land) at Raumati and Omaha beaches, both in New Zealand, coincided with the subdivision of the land for

housing (Gibb, 1978; Healy, 1981). Erosion rates on the Outer Banks of North Carolina, USA, have often been faster where human interference of the natural condition has occurred, as it has on the coral cays of the Caribbean (Dolan *et al.,* 1973; Stoddart, 1963).

Many coastal areas are among the most heavily utilized parts of the land surface. Port facilities, industrial sites and towns are just some of the established features that may occur. The coast as a recreation and leisure area generates additional human pressures and modifications. There are many examples in the literature of the battle to prevent or lessen erosion – to maintain the *status quo* – and of attempts to provide the data which might form the basis of long-term management plans (Hails, 1977; Clayton, 1980; Nordstrom and Allen, 1980; Jolliffe, 1983; Carter, 1988).

Rarely, however, have the consequences of human activity at the coast resulted in such major losses or additions of land as might happen if there should be a rise in sea level as a result of human induced atmospheric warming. Far more often human action has only tended to hasten those natural processes that are already operating. Dramatic as many of the changes have been, the majority of them cannot be considered to be as important and as potentially damaging as, for example, the effects wrought by pollution in the Mediterranean or in the North Sea.

Slope modification

As surface dwellers the impact of human beings upon the morphology of the land has been widespread, yet it is suggested here that, as in the case of coasts, most of the changes to slopes have been very minor in relation to the scale of the natural land surface. As at the coast, human interference with slopes tends to have been most effective in speeding up naturally occurring processes rather than in creating major new features.

An example of rapid and widespread changes to the land surface being induced by human action is seen in areas of soil erosion (chapter 3). At its most dramatic, slopes are scarred by shallow slips (plate 7), yet in the majority of cases the underlying slope form remains. The same may be said of the soil conservation technique which involves the grading of slopes to reduce soil

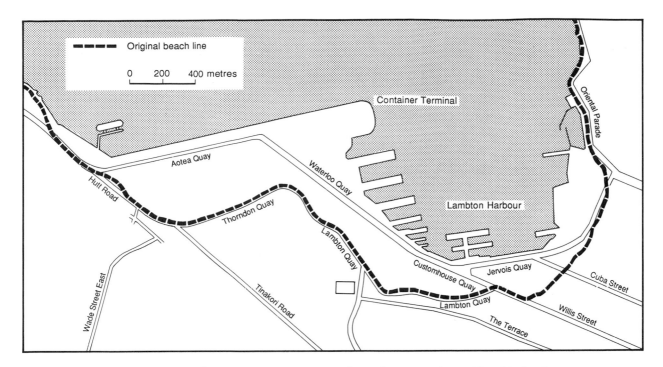

Figure 10   The original (1840) and the present shore of Wellington harbour, New Zealand.
Source: Mulgan (1939) and others

erosion. Even the technique of terracing which, in areas such as the Philippines, China, the Mediterranean Basin and the Rhine Gorge, forms such striking landscapes, rarely obscures the basic slope.

In urban areas the intensity of slope modification is often very high indeed, given the necessity for buildings and roads to be constructed on sound engineering principles. Almost all buildings with foundations cause some modification to the natural slope of the land and even on flat sites large modern buildings often involve the removal of material to allow for proper foundations and underground car parks to be incorporated. Slope modification tends to increase as construction moves onto steeper slopes. In these circumstances, to provide a horizontal base plus reasonable access, a cut-and-fill technique is often used, thereby creating a small, level terrace with over-steepened slopes at both ends. The steep cut-slopes, devoid of soil and vegetation, are potentially much less stable than the former natural slopes and during times of intense rainfall are susceptible to small but quite damaging land slips. In the winter of 1976, a total of 1149 slips was recorded in Wellington, New Zealand, yet beyond the urban area slope failures were rare (Eyles *et al.*, 1978). Comparable effects have been noted in Los Angeles by Cooke (1984) and in Hong Kong by Lumb (1975).

Modern technology can greatly reduce the dangers as was shown in Los Angeles where over 90% of the nearly 3000 slope failures affecting property occurred in pre-1963 developments (Cooke, 1984). A summary of the literature is provided by Alexander (1989).

Probably the largest changes to slopes have been the result of mining and quarrying activities. Among the largest holes are the Bingham Canyon copper mine in Utah, USA, which is over 775 m deep and covers over 7.2 km^2, and the open-cast lignite mine near Bergheim, West Germany, which is 325 m deep and extends over 21 km^2. In Britain, the Old Delabole slate quarry in Cornwall is over 150 m deep and has a circumference of 26 km. Spoil tips, although smaller, are often more intrusive in the landscape. Many rise 30–40 m above the surrounding area.

In recent years many holes and tips have proved to be transient features of the land surface as the demand for landfill sites has increased and uses for spoil have been developed. In contrast some holes and tips have become an integral part of the leisure industry. In the UK, the Broads in Norfolk and Suffolk, formed from earlier peat diggings, is one such example, and the wet gravel pits of the Lea valley in Hertfordshire which now form an important water-based leisure park, are another.

Subsidence

Slope modification is not always brought about by action at the surface. There are a growing number of instances where quite extensive subsidence has occurred following either the removal of subterranean solids for example coal and salt, or the removal of subterranean fluids such as water, oil and gases. Subsidence may also be induced by surface loading and other compaction-inducing processes such as hydrocompaction, vibration and land drainage (Carbognin, 1985; Coates, 1983; Holzner, 1984; Poland, 1984; Ireland *et al.*, 1984; Ghetti and Batisse, 1983; Doidge, 1982).

The effects of subsidence can result in vertical lowering of the surface, tilting, breaks in the ground (fissuring) and subsurface deformation. Worldwide, the direct and indirect costs related to subsidence run into millions of pounds each year (Coates, 1979). Among damage due to subsidence one may cite broken dams, cracked buildings, offset roads and railways, and deformed irrigation ditches. Subsidence also affects natural features and may cause the ponding of water as indicated in the 'flashes' of Cheshire, England, changes in river flow regimes and an increased incidence of loading as has been recorded in the Santa Clara and San Joaquin Valleys in California (Poland *et al.*, 1975; Bell, 1975).

In some senses the amount of damage caused by subsidence is out of all proportion to the amount of surface change that takes place. Clearly very slight movement of the land beneath a structure's foundations can be extremely damaging. This is exemplified by the damage to buildings caused by the movement consequent upon the drying out of clay soils and rocks during the dry summers of 1989 and 1990 in Britain. By far the most obvious subsidence effects are the dramatic small-scale sinkholes that sometimes occur in areas underlaid by limestone or dolomite. Collapse in these areas has been occasioned, for example, by the removal of underground water to allow miners access to mineralized zones (in adjacent or lower strata). Thus, dewatering of a gold mining area near Johannesburg lowered the aquifer by between 100 and 550 m. Between 1962 and 1966 eight sinkholes formed, the largest of which was 125 m across and 50 m in depth, as underground arches collapsed following the removal of the supporting water (Beguidenhout and Enslin, 1970).

Once formed, sinkholes are a distinctive feature of the land surface. However, in very many examples of subsidence the vertical component is very small compared with the horizontal component, as table 5 shows.

In these circumstances the effects of subsidence on the land are often undetectable to the casual observer. Examples of large-scale, low-amplitude subsidence include the Houston–Galveston area of Texas, an area of 12,170 km² which has sunk a maximum of 2.75 m due to groundwater extraction, the Long Beach area of California, an area of 78 km² which has sunk a maximum of 8.8 m, and the Venice area of Italy which has sunk 0.14 m (Gabrysch, 1980; Mayuga and Allen, 1970; Carbognin *et al.*, 1977; Doidge, 1982).

Table 5 Horizontal and vertical changes in selected areas of subsidence

Name of locality	Maximum subsidence (m)	Horizontal component (area affected (km²))	Cause
San Joaquin Valley	9.0	13,500	groundwater extraction
Tokyo area, Japan	4.6	400	groundwater extraction
Lake Maracaibo, Venezuela	3.9	50	oil wells
Wilmington, Long Beach, California	8.8	78	oil and gas wells
London, UK	0.35	450	groundwater extraction

Source: Poland *et al.* (1975)

Table 6 Deaths by volcanic hazards, 1600–1982

Hazard	No. of deaths	%
Lava flows	985	0.4
Tephra falls and volcanic bombs	10,953	4.6
Pyroclastic flows and debris avalanches	54,995	23.0
Lahars and jokulhlaups	14,746	6.2
Seismic activity	89	0.04
Tsunami	44,356	18.6
Atmospheric effects	63	0.03
Gases and acid rain	185	0.08
Disease and starvation	95,313	39.9
Unknown	17,182	7.2
Total	238,867	100

Source: Blong (1984)

In Britain extraction of water from the chalk aquifer under London is thought to have been responsible for causing subsidence over a 450 km² area with a maximum amount of 0.35 m. Another example is provided by the peatlands of East Anglia where the gradual emergence of the Holme Post in the fens of Huntingdonshire, established as a fixed datum point in 1840 against which peat subsidence could be recorded, is well documented (Hutchinson, 1980; Cooke and Doornkamp, 1990). The overall lowering in the past 140 years amounts to almost 4.0 m. This rate has not been constant but phased with the installation of pumps nearby (Hutchinson, 1980).

Hazard warning

Along with an increased capability to bring about change to the land surface has gone an increased understanding of the natural processes operating upon the surface. This has made it possible, in some cases, to model the location and extent of the changes before they occur and with this knowledge to plan the location and scale of new developments where they will cause least damage and be least vulnerable. This greater understanding may also permit action to be taken once development is occurring, that will lessen the predicted effects. The recharging of reservoir rocks following oil and water extraction is one example. A further benefit is that remedial planning and subsequent action

can be undertaken before the changes lead to a catastrophe. Protection works such as the Lower Thames Barrier near London or the Dutch Delta Plan provide examples.

Recognition of a potential threat, whether caused directly by human action as in cases of subsidence or whether related to a natural event, such as a storm or hurricane, a flood or a tsunami, at least gives the opportunity to formulate plans to lessen the impact. Slopes (Hansen, 1984), coasts (Gibb, 1983), and rivers (Smith and Tobin, 1979) have all seen major advances in this field. The mitigation of volcanic and earthquake hazards is another important area.

Volcanic hazards

Deaths from volcanic activity, either direct or indirect, since 1600 are estimated at almost 260,000 (Blong, 1984). Death can occur from a variety of causes. Lava flows, although destructive, rarely cause a high death toll because, once established, they are relatively predictable. Volcanic 'bombs' and tephra falls, although less predictable, also rarely result in major deaths even though the economic damage of ash falls may be substantial. Far more hazardous are the pyroclastic flows and debris avalanches (table 6).

The death toll following the pyroclastic flow at Mt Pelee in 1902, on the island of Martinique, is put at between 25,000 and 30,000, making it one of the most devastating eruptions ever. The Unzen eruption of 1792 in Japan may have caused over 14,000 deaths, while the Taal volcano in the Philippines may have killed more than the 1335 reported deaths in 1911. The eruption of Mt St Helens in 1980 resulted in more than 50 deaths by pyroclastic flows out of a total number of 60.

Although constrained to some extent by the form of the land, lahars – mudflows containing debris and angular blocks of predominantly volcanic origin – quite commonly kill small numbers of people and occasionally many more. The outburst at Galunggung, West Java, in 1822 reportedly resulted in 3,600 deaths and that at Kelut in 1919, 5,110. Possibly six of those killed at Mt St Helens died in lahars.

Volcanic gases might easily be dismissed as an improbable danger to human life, having accounted for only 0.08% of all deaths between 1900 and 1982. Yet in 1986 over 1,000 people died in the Cameroons when a large bubble of volcanic gas escaped suddenly from Lake Nyos (*The Times*, 25 August 1986).

In the past by far the largest number of deaths associated with volcanism have resulted from drowning by tsunamis or from starvation following the smothering of crops and grass with tephra. Over 30,000 people are thought to have died by drowning following the Krakatoa eruption in 1883.

Modern food-aid and distribution techniques should prevent further significant deaths by starvation, and the existence of the Honolulu-based Tsunami Warning System ought to alert people around the Pacific to the dangers of a tsunami and help reduce casualities from this source. As far as actual volcanoes are concerned greater safety can be obtained by simply recording the pattern of past eruptions and noting their dates, mode of eruption and the localities affected. Analysis of this type of data in conjunction with detailed topographic maps of the area can help pin-point areas of special risk. Technical analysis of the volcano – measuring gas emissions, water temperature, gravity, earthquake activity and angular changes of the surface, now using laser techniques – can help give warning of a forthcoming eruption.

Intensive monitoring is expensive and, bearing in mind that there are over 850 active volcanoes in the world, it is clear that resources have to be concentrated on the potentially most damaging sites. Japanese, Italian and American studies are especially important in this connection as are the less sophisticated methods used in Indonesia where 77 of its volcanoes have erupted in historic time.

Closely allied to preparing hazard maps, monitoring volcanic events, and giving actual warning is the assessment of the potential impact of volcanic hazards in terms of possible death and injuries, damage to dwellings and commercial buildings, and effects on agriculture and other economic activities. This has important implications for any disaster relief plan that is drawn up and for future planning within the area. One of the few important studies of this nature has been carried out in the Raboul area of Papua New Guinea (Blong and Aislabie, 1988).

Earthquake hazards

Human response to earthquakes and earthquake risk should be in a similar vein to that adopted for volcanic action. In other words there is a need to monitor areas of potential activity, to plan and design for eventualities and to react to events during and after an earthquake. One example where intense efforts have been made in this direction is in the Parkfield area of California (see pages 54 and 55).

There are examples of earth tremors being caused by human action. Those associated with the underground testing of nuclear bombs are well known. So too are the tremors associated with the creation of large reservoirs such as those impounded by the Hoover dam (USA), the Kariba dam (Zimbabwe), the Kremasta dam (Greece), and the Koyna dam (India). In each of these examples the impounding of the water led to numerous tremors, the largest of which exceeded 5.0 on the Richter scale (Judd, 1974; Bolt *et al.*, 1975). In the case of the Koyna dam 177 people were killed. Not all dams cause tremors. The geological conditions are important, particularly the degree of stress already applied to the rocks, but so too is the ground-water condition since tremors are more common when the impounded water is in hydraulic continuity with the ground water. Other causes of earthquakes include the excavation of mines, which again relates closely to the stress condition of the rocks, and the injection of fluids into pores and cracks (Gough, 1978).

For the most part, however, the human response to earthquakes is a reactive one. As the structure of the Earth has been unravelled, the location of areas most at risk to earthquakes has become known in some detail. However, very few areas have adopted significant remedial measures. Thus, earthquakes are still a major killer, as the Armenian earthquake of 1988 demonstrated with 25,000 people killed and the 1990 Iranian earthquake showed with perhaps 30,000 killed.

Yet it is possible to reduce the damage and loss of life using modern technology. This was shown by the 7.1 force San Francisco earthquake of October 1989 which killed just 62 people and caused damage put at £3 billion. Considerable advances have been made in determining quite accurately where an earthquake is likely to occur. Identifying when movement will occur remains for the future. Both the identification of the general area at earthquake risk and the more detailed location at risk rely on geological and geophysical evidence. It is geophysical data too that is used to determine within the detailed locations those areas that appear to be at risk in the short term. In other words it is possible to identify areas where one can reasonably expect there will be an earthquake before too long, even though precisely forecasting its occurrence is not yet possible. This involves identifying areas within a belt of seismic activity that have not experienced an earthquake, that is areas known as seismic gaps.

Since the concept of the seismic gap is relatively new there are relatively few examples to show how successful it is as a predictor. However, a major earthquake in 1985 occurred in the Michoacan seismic gap in Mexico (Degg, 1986), and there is some evidence that an earthquake will take place near Parkfield, California, before 1993 (Roy, 1990). Recognition of an earthquake cycle of about 22 years duration in the area lies at the root of the study and has prompted seismologists to establish an arsenal of monitoring equipment. Seismometers will measure microquakes and earth tremors, creep meters will document fault slippage, borehole strainmeters will measure rock deformation, magnetometers will chronicle changes in the Earth's magnetic field, dilatometers will record expansion and compression in rocks, while laser beams will measure ground displacement. The whole area has been linked to an alarm system with a view to giving 72 hours' warning of the next shock (Bakum, 1988a, 1988b; Sherburne, 1988; Bakum *et al.*, 1987).

The intensity of this instrumentation should greatly increase the understanding of earthquakes in general, provided one occurs, and hence allow other potential sites to be studied more effectively. In a highly built-up area like California accurate forecasting of a tremor could save many lives.

However, knowing when an earthquake will occur is only one aspect of the topic since this will not, in itself, reduce damage. Damage limitation can be achieved best by adopting the most appropriate land use, by land zoning and by applying appropriate building standards. Areas of rock and soil that are especially susceptible to ground movement such as soft sandstone, marine sands, alluvium and, especially, artificially reclaimed land should be avoided, as should sites actually on, or close to, active faults. An important strategy is to specify risk-reducing building standards through local governmental building codes and to ensure that the codes are enforced (Andrews and Goltz, 1988). Careful preparation and rehearsal of disaster plans and the maintenance of rescue services can also greatly reduce deaths, injuries and damage to property (Bakum, 1988c).

Unlike other examples included in this *Update*, earthquakes are an almost wholly negative feature of the natural environment. They may cause death and destruction and the landforms created are rarely more useful than those that existed before the movement. One earthquake that did have some positive aspect was the 1855 Wellington earthquake in New Zealand, which led to a rise in the land area, and in the shore platform in particular, of about 1.5 m. This rise greatly improved the access to the Hutt Valley from Wellington by providing a cliff-foot strip of land just above the level of wave action (Stevens, 1974).

Endpiece

The previous sections have noted the value to human beings of the components of the natural environment, and some of the ways in which the climate, vegetation, soils and landforms have been used, modified and misused. One point to emerge is that human influence on the environment is not a new phenomenon. What is new, however, is the capacity that now exists to bring about change (witness the speed with which tropical forests are being cleared), the complexity of many of the changes now occurring as a consequence of technological innovations (the links between

Case study: the Parkfield story

Location of Parkfield.

The background

Parkfield, population 34, is a small settlement in central California almost midway between San Francisco and Los Angeles. In April 1985 the US Geological Survey issued a prediction that an earthquake of approximately magnitude 6 would occur before 1993 near Parkfield. This is the first officially recognized scientific prediction of an earthquake in the United States. One million US dollars of State funds and a further one million US dollars of Federal funds have been provided to build the geophysical instrumentation in the area to the point where the Parkfield section of the San Andreas fault is without doubt the most densely and comprehensively instrumented earthquake source region in the world. There is a twofold aim. The first is to obtain a detailed understanding of the geological processes that precede the anticipated earthquake in the hope that this knowledge can be applied to other areas of significant seismic hazard. The second, and secondary, goal is to issue a short-term warning of the anticipated quake.

The history

The San Andreas fault separates the Pacific plate from the North American plate. Since the Pacific plate is moving the faster, there is slippage between them. In general terms this averages about 10 mm per year but, in practice, conditions are so variable this is not a very helpful figure. More important is the fact that movement between crustal plates often produces earthquakes and, indeed, California is noted for earthquakes, perhaps the most famous being the 1906 San Franciscan earthquake of 8.3 magnitude.

Geophysical conditions along the San Andreas fault vary. North-west of Parkfield the fault line is highly mobile, movement occurring as a seismic fault creep. As a consequence little, if any, strain accumulates and hence powerful earthquake shocks (in excess of magnitude 6) are unknown. South-east of Parkfield the two plates appear to be locked together. Hence strain builds between the two until there is a sudden unlocking accompanied by a large earthquake (more than magnitude 7). The Parkfield area lies transitional between the two in as much as strain gradually builds and is released by an earthquake of approximately magnitude 6. Significantly the strain-building period is about 21 or 22 years. Hence there exists the possibility of monitoring the build-up towards an earthquake. In the past earthquakes have occurred in 1966, 1934, 1922, 1901, 1881 and 1857. There is a 0.9 (90%) probability that the next will occur before 1993. Nowhere else along the San Andreas fault can a probability of more than 0.5 (50%) be determined.

The instrumentation

The geophysical instrumentation operated by the US Geological Survey, and others, near Parkfield is designed to monitor ongoing tectonic processes that generate earthquakes, and to record any

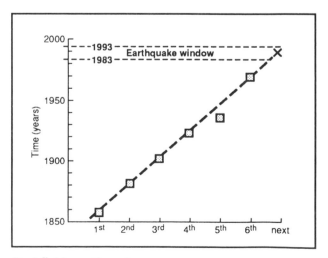

Parkfield: earthquake occurrence.

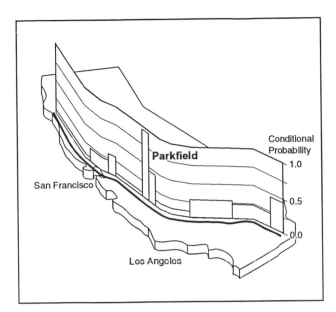

Fence diagram to show probability for occurrence of major earthquakes along the San Andreas fault 1988–2018.

shaking and its effects. Seismicity in the area is being monitored by more than 200 seismometers and accelerometers. 116 of these have been fixed in a single 1.5 km deep well drilled near the fault. Creep is being recorded on 13 creep meters of which 11 have a 0.02 mm resolution. A variety of strain meters (dilatometers), 11 in all, have been deployed to monitor deformation, while four closely spaced, shallow, borehole tiltmeters measure tilt. Eighteen wells have been constructed to measure fluctuations in ground water level. Field magnetometers have been set up at seven sites. Instruments are also available to measure any changes in electrical Earth currents and in Earth resistivity while an 81 KH$_z$ radio frequency monitor will test for electromagnetic emission. Laser-based surveying techniques have established a geodimeter network to measure ground deformation over a wider area.

Hazard warning
Most of the effort at Parkfield is directed at improving our understanding of earthquakes so that useful measurements can be made elsewhere in the future. However, there is also the aim of developing an early warning system based upon the monitoring. If anomalies appear in the continuous analysis of the data, then an alert is issued, with grade E representing the normal conditions and grades D through to A representing increasing levels of alert. A public warning will be issued when a level A alert is declared indicating that there is a more than 37% chance of an earthquake occurring within the next 72 hours. Issuing an alert is one thing, making use of the time is quite another, and at Parkfield a significant effort has been made between the scientists and the local administrators to ensure a response to a prediction, not just to an event.

automobile emissions and acid rain, and of CFCs upon ozone concentrations provide examples), and the sheer intensity of human action as a consequence of the growth in global population (Hall, 1990). Following on from the last of these developments is the fact that the human species has so successfully colonized this planet that there is now little opportunity to withdraw from a major settled area to allow it time to recover. Several of the effects of human action are for the first time regional and even trans-national in extent.

Recent technological and scientific developments have enabled us to understand more clearly the workings of the natural environment, to foresee the consequences of a particular course of action, to restrict, if not eliminate, the major dangers to the environment and to repair some, at least, of the past damage. No less importantly, science and technology can now assist in achieving a sustainable level of production much higher than only 30 years ago. It is increasingly recognized that environmental degradation, in the widest sense, derives from social, economic and political considerations. The emergence of the notion 'the polluter pays' and the call, sometimes made, for an environmental impact assessment before embarking on a major development project, together with the growing number of people who are interested in, and concerned about, the environment, point to a developing awareness of its importance. Such an awareness is still in its infancy and in the meantime the pace of environmental change quickens and world population increases.

Bibliography

Agassi, M., Shainberg, I., Warrington, D. and Ben-hur, M. (1989) Run-off and erosion control in potato fields, *Soil Science*, **148**, 149–154

Alexander, D. (1989) Urban landslides, *Progress in Physical Geography*, **13**, 157–191

Allen, O.E. (1983) *Atmosphere*, Time-Life Books, Amsterdam

Andrews, R. and Goltz, J. (1988) State public policy issues with the Parkfield prediction experiment, *Earthquakes and Volcanoes*, **20**, 87–91

Bagnall, A.G. (1976) *Wairarapa: an Historical Excursion*, Hedley's Bookshop, Masterton, New Zealand

Bakum, W.H. (1988a) History of significant earthquakes in the Parkfield area, *Earthquakes and Volcanoes*, **20**, 45–51

Bakum, W.H. (1988b) Geophysical instrumentation near Parkfield, *Earthquake and Volcanoes*, **20**, 83–86

Bakum, W.H. (1988c) The USGS plan for short-term prediction of the anticipated Parkfield earthquake, *Earthquakes and Volcanoes*, **20**, 83–86

Bakum, W.H. *et al.* (1987) Parkfield, California earthquake prediction scenarios and response plans, *US Geol Surv. Open-File Report,* 87–192

Balchin, W.G.V. (ed.) (1971) *Swansea and its Region,* Brit. Assoc. Ad. Sci.

Barney, G.O. (1980) *The Global 2000 Report to the President of the US*, Pergamon, New York

Barr, B.M. and Braden K.E. (1987) *The Disappearing Russian Forest. A Dilemma in Soviet Resource Management,* Rowan and Littlefield, London

Battarbee, R. *et al.* (1989) Geographical research on acid rain, *Geogr. Jl.*, **155**, 353–377

Beguidenhout, C.A. and Enslin, J.F. (1970) Surface subsidences in the dolomite areas of the Far West Rand, Transvaal, Republic of South Africa, *Int. Ass. of Scientific Hydrology,* Pub. No. 89, 482–95

Bell, F.G. (1975) Salt and subsidence in Cheshire, England. *Engineering Geology*, **9**, 237–47

Bennett, H.H. (1939) *Soil Conservation,* McGraw Hill, New York, 993

Bernhardson, W. (1986) Campesinos and conservation in the central Andes: indigenous herding and conserving the vicuna, *Environmental Conservation*, **13**, 311–18

Beveridge, A.E. and Herbert, J. (1978) Selected logging trials and their implication for forest management in the west Taupo forests, Indigenous Silviculture Report No. 20, New Zealand Forest Service, Forest Research Institute, Unpublished

Blaikie, P. (1985) *The Political Economy of Soil Erosion in Developing Countries*, Longman, London

Blong, R. (1966) Discontinuous gullies on the Volcanic Plateau, *New Zealand Journal of Hydrology,* **5**, 87–99

Blong, R. (1970) The development of discontinuous gullies in a pumice catchment *Am. J. Sci.*, **268**, 369–83

Blong, R. (1984) *Volcanic Hazards*, Academic Press, Sydney, Australia

Blong, R.J. and Aislabie, C. (1988) *The Impact of Volcanic Hazards at Raboul, Papua, New Guinea*, Discussion Paper No. 33, Institute of National Affairs, Port Moresby

Boardman, J. (1989) *Soil Erosion in Britain: Costs, Attitudes and Policies,* Social Audit Paper No. 1, 28, University of Sussex, Education Network for Environment and Development

Boardman, J., Dearing, J. and Foster, I. (1990) *Soil Erosion on Agricultural Land,* John Wiley, Chichester, 640

Boardman, J. and Robinson, D.A. (1985) Soil erosion, climatic vagary and agricultural change in the Downs around Lewes and Brighton, autumn 1982, *Applied Geography,* **5**, 243–58

Bolt, B.A., Horn, W.L. (1975) Hazards from earthquakes, in Bolt, B.A., Macdonald, G.A. and Springer-Scott, R.F. *et al.* (eds.), *Geological Hazards*, Springer-Verlag, New York, 1–62

Brady, N. (1990) *The Nature and Properties of Soils*, Maxwell Macmillan, New York

Bredemier, M. (1990) Nature and potential of ecosystem internal acidification processes in relation to acid deposition, in Longhurst, J.W.S. (ed.) *Acid Deposition: Sources, Effects and Controls*, British Library Technical Communication, 197–212

Buckham, A.F. and Cockfield, W.E. (1950) Gullies formed by sinking of the ground, *Am. J. Sci.*, **248**, 137–141

Buckland, M. (1988) Landscape: a basis for town and country planning, *Planning Quarterly* (New Zealand), **92**, 20–24

Burt, S. and Mansfield, D. (1988) The great storm of 15–16 October 1987, *Weather*, **43**, 90–110

Carbognin, L. (1985) Land subsidence: a worldwide environmental hazard, *Nature and Resources*, **21**, 2–11

Carbognin, L., Gatto, P. and Mozzi, G. (1977) New trends in the subsidence of Venice, *Inst. Ass. of Scientific Hydrology*, Pub. No. 121, 65–81

Carter, R.W.G. (1988) *Coastal Environment*, Academic Press, London

Chandler, T.J. (1965) *The Climate of London*, Hutchinson, London

Clayton, K.M. (1980) Coastal protection along the East Anglian coast, UK, *Zeit für Geom., Supp. vol.* **34**, 142–154

Cloutman, E.W. and Smith, A.G. (1988) Palaeo-environments in the Vale of Pickering, Pt. 3, Environmental history at Star Carr, *Proc. Prehist. Soc.*, **54**, 37–58

Coates, D.R. (1980) Subsidence influences, in K.J. Gregory and D.E. Walling (eds.), *Man and Environmental Processes*, Dawson and Sons, Folkestone, Kent, 163–168

Coates, D.R. (1983) Large-scale land subsidence, in Gardner, R. and Scoging, H. (eds.), *Mega-Geomorphology,* OUP, Oxford, 212–233

Cochrane, G.R. (1969) Problems of vegetation change in western Viti Levu, Fiji, in Gale, F. and Lawton, G., (eds.), *Settlement and Encounter,* 115–147

Colborne, G.J.N. and Staines, S.J. (1985) Soil erosion in Somerset and Dorset *South East England Soils Discussion Group*, **3**, 62–71

Cooke, R.U. (1984) *Geomorphological Hazards in Los Angeles*, Allen and Unwin, London

Cooke, R.U. and Doornkamp, J. (1974) *Geomorphology in Environmental Management*, Clarendon Press, Oxford

Cooke, R.U. and Doornkamp, K.C. (1990) *Geomorphology in Environmental Management: a New Introduction*, 2nd edn, OUP, Oxford

Cowan, P., Atkinson, I. and Bell, B. (1985) Kapiti Island - the last possum, *Forest and Bird*, **16**, 12–13

58

Crozier, M.J. *et al.* (1980) Distribution of landslips in the Wairarapa Lill Country, *NZ Journal of Geology and Geophysics*, **23**, 575–586

Cruickshank, J.G. (1972) Soils and changing agricultural land values in part of Co. Londonderry, *Irish Geographer*, **6**, 462–479

Cumberland, K.B. (1981) *Landmarks*, Readers Digest Services PTY Limited, Australia

Darby, H.C. (1951) The changing English landscape, *Geog. J.*, **117**, 377–398

Degg, M. (1986) *The 1985 Mexican Earthquake*, Re-insurance Offices Association, London

Dent, D. and Young, A. (1981) *Soil Survey and Land Evaluation,* George Allen & Unwin, London

Doidge, P. (1982) The drowning of Venice, *New Scientist* **94**, (1310), 790–791

Dolan, R., Godfrey, P. and Odum, W. (1973) Man's impact on the barrier islands of North Carolina, *American Scientist* **60** (6), 152–166

Douglas, I. (1967) Natural and man-made erosion in the humid tropics of Australia, Malaysia and Singapore, *Int. Assoc. Scient. Hydrol.*, **75**, 17–30

Eckholm, E., Foley, G., Barnard, G. and Timberlake, L. (1984) *Fuelwood: the Energy Crisis That Won't Go Away*, Earthscan, London

Eden, P. (1988) Hurricane Gilbert, *Weather*, **43**, 446–448

Elsom, D. (1987) *Atmospheric Pollution*, Basil Blackwell, Oxford.

Evans, B. (1988) Some effects of soil erosion in Britain, *Geography Review*, **2**, 34–37

Evans, R. (1980) Characteristics of water-eroded fields in lowland England, in De Boodk, M. and Gabriel, D. (eds.), *Assessment of Erosion*, John Wiley, Chichester

Evans, R. (1990) Water erosion in British farmers' fields: some causes, impacts, predictions, *Prog. in Phys. Geog.*, **14**, 199–219

Evans, R. and Cook, S. (1986) Soil erosion in Britain, *South East England Soils Discussion Group*, **3**, 28–58

Evans, R. and Northcliffe, S. (1978) Soil erosion in North Norfolk, *Journal of Agricultural Science* (Cambridge) **90**, 185–192

Eyles, G.O. (1987) *Soil erosion in the South Pacific,* Environmental Studies Report, University of South Pacific, Institute of Natural Resources, **27**

Eyles, R.J., Crozier, M.J. and Wheeler, R.H. (1978) Landslips in Wellington City, *New Zealand Geographer*, **34**, 58–74

FAO (Food and Agriculture Organization) (1961) Forestry News Letter of the Near East, FAO, Regional Office, Cairo

FAO (1985) *Fuelwood and Energy. Priority Action in Tropical Forestry*, FAO Forestry Department (draft working paper), Rome

FAO/UNEP (United Nations Environmental Programme) (1982) *Tropical Forest Resources*, by J.P. Lanley, FAO Forestry Papers No. 30, Rome

Gabrysch, R.K. (1980) *Approximate Land Surface Subsidence in the Houston-Galveston Region, Texas, 1906–78, 1943–78, and 1973–78*, US Geological Survey Open File Report, No. 80–338

Ghetti, A. and Balisse, M. (1983) The overall protection of Venice and its lagoon, *Nature and Resources*, **19**, 7–19

Gibb, J. (1978) *The Problem of Coastal Erosion along the 'Golden Coast', Western Wellington, New Zealand*, Water and Soil Tech Publ, No. 10, NWASCO

Gibb, J.G. (1983) Combating coastal erosion by the technique of coastal hazard mapping, *New Zealand Engineering*, **38**, 15–19

Gifford, J. (1953) Landslides on Exmoor caused by the storm of 15th August 1952, *Geography*, **38**, 9–17

Goudie, A. (1981) *The Human Impact: Man's Role in Environmental Change*, Blackwell, Oxford

Gough, D.I. (1978) Induced seismicity, in: *The Assessment and Mitigation of Earthquake Risk*, UNESCO, Paris, 91–117

Grayson, L. (1989) *Acid Rain and the Environment, 1984–1988, a Select Bibliography*, British Library Science Reference and Information Service

Hails, J.R. (1977) Applied geomorphology in coastal-zone planning and management, in Hails, J.R. (ed.), *Applied Geomorphology*, Elsevier, Amsterdam

Halford, J. (1986) Germany's forests are dying, *Plain Truth*, **51**, 15–16, 24

Hall, J., Barnard, G. and Moss, P. (1982) *Biomass Energy in the Developing Countries*, Pergamon, Oxford

Hall, R. (1990) *World Population Trends*, CUP, Cambridge

Hansen, A. (1984) Landslide hazard analysis, in Brunsden, D. and Prior, D.B. (eds.), *Slope Instability*, John Wiley, Chichester, 523–602

Harant, H. and Jarry, D. (1967) *Guide du naturaliste dans le Midi de la France. II La garrigue, le maquis, les cultures*, Neuchâtel, Paris

Havens, B.S. *et al.* (1978) *Early History of Cloud Seeding*, State University of New York, Albany

Healy, T.R. (1981) Mistakes at Omaha, *Soil and Water*, **17**, 22–25

Herbert, J. and Beveridge, A.E. (1977) A selective logging trial in dense podocarp forest in the central North Island, *NZ Journal of Forestry*, **22**, 81–100

Hodges, R.D. and Arden-Clarke, C. (1986) *Soil Erosion in Britain*, The Soil Association, Bristol,

Holland, P. (1988) Plants and lowland South Canterbury landscapes, *New Zealand Geographer*, **44**, 50–60

Holzner, T.L. (ed.) (1984) Man-induced land subsidence, *Geol. Soc. Am.; Reviews in Engineering Geology No. 6*

Howard, G. (1970) A paradox of plenty. Soil erosion and soil and water resources in New Zealand, *Proc. NZ Water Conference*, Part 1, 4.1–4.20

Hudson, N.W. (1971) *Soil Conservation*, Cornell Univ. Press, Ithaca, NY

Hudson, N.W. (1981) *Soil Conservation*, 2nd edn, Cornell Univ. Press, Ithaca, NY

Hull, A. (1986) How Provence burned, *Geographical Mag.*, **58** (11), 550–552

Hutchinson, J.N. (1980) The record of peat wastage in the East Anglian fenlands at Holme Post 1848–1978 AD, *J. Ecol.*, **68**, 229–249

Innes, J.L. (1989) Acid rain: and trees. In Longhurst, J.W.S. (ed.), *Acid Depositions: Sources, Effects and Controls*, British Library Technical Communications, 229–241

Ireland, R.L., Poland, J.F. and Riley, F.S. (1984) *Land subsidence in the San Joaquin Valley California as of 1980*, US Geol. Surv.– Prof. Paper, 437–1

James, I. (1990) Possum peril, *Forest and Bird*, **21**, 30–33

Jolliffe, I.P. (1983) Coastal erosion and flood abatement. What are the options? *Geog. J.*, **149**, 62–71

Jones, D.K.C. (1973) Man moulds the landscape, *Geographical Mag.*, **45** (8), 575–581

Jones, D.K.C. *et al.* (1983) A preliminary geomorphological assessment of the Karakoram Highway, *Quart. Jl. Eng. Geol.*, **16**, 331–355

Judd, W.R. (1974) Seismic effects of reservoir impounding, *Engineering Geology*, **8**, 1–22

Laffen, M.D. *et al.* (1977) Landscapes, soils, and erosion in a catchment in the Wither Hills, Marlborough, *NZ J. Sci.*, **20**, 279–289

Liedke, H (1989) Soil erosion and soil removal in Fiji, *Applied Geography and Development*, **33**, 68–92

Lumb, P. (1975) Slope failures in Hong Kong, *Quart. Jl. Eng. Geol.*, **8**, 31–65

MacLean, H. (1982) Lake Wairarapa: poldly onwards? *Soil and Water*, **18**, 10–13

Madeley, J. (1988) People transplanted, forests uprooted, *Geographical Mag.*, **60** (7), 22–25

Malanson, G.P. (1985) Fire management in coastal sage-scrub, southern California, USA, *Environmental Conservation*, **12**, 141–146

Marsh, G.P. (1864) *Man and Nature; or, Physical Geography as Modified by Human Actions*, Scribners, New York

Mason, B.J. (1966) The role of meteorology in the national economy, *Weather*, **21**, 51–57

Mason, B.J. (1990) Acid rain – cause and consequence, *Weather*, **45**, 70–79

Mather, A.S. (1987) Global trends in forest resources, *Geog.*, **72**, 1–15

Maunder, W.J. (1966) Climatic variations and agricultural production in New Zealand, *New Zealand Geographer*, **22**, 55–69

Maunder, W.J. (1970) *The Value of Weather*, Methuen, London

Maunder, W.J. (1971) *The Economic Consequences of Drought: with Particular Reference to the 1969/70 Drought in New Zealand*, New Zealand Meteorological Service Technical Note No. 192

Maunder, W.J. (1986) *The Uncertainty Business*, Methuen, London

Maunder, W.J. (1989) *The Human Impact of Climatic Uncertainty*, Routledge, London

Maunder, W.J. and Ausubel, J.H. (1985) Identifying climatic sensitivity, in Kates, R.W., Ausubel, J.H. and Berberian, M. (eds.), *Climate Impact Assessment. Studies of the Interaction of Climate and Society*, SCOPE 27, Wiley, New York, 85–104

Mayuga, M.N. and Allen, D.R. (1970) Subsidence in the Wilmington oil field, Long Beach, California, *Int. Ass. of Scientific Hydrology*, Pub. No. 89, 66–79

McCaskill, L.W. (1969) *Molesworth*, A.H. and A.W. Reed, Wellington, New Zealand

McCaskill, L.W. (1973) *Hold this Land*, A.H and A.W. Reed, Wellington, New Zealand

Moore, N. (1962) The heaths of Dorset and their conservation, *J. L. Ecol.*, **50**, 369–391

Morgan, R.P.C. (1977) *Soil Erosion in the United Kingdom: Field Studies in the Silsoe Area, 1973–75*, National College of Agricultural Engineering, Silsoe, Occ. Paper No. 4

Morgan, R.P.C. (1979) *Soil Erosion*, Longman, London

Morgan, R.P.C. (1979) Soil erosion measurement and soil conservation research in cultivated areas of the UK *Geographical Journal*, **151**, 11–20

Morgan, R.P.C., Martin, L. and Noble, C.A. (1987) *Soil Erosion in the United Kingdom: a Case Study from Mid-Bedfordshire*, National College of Agricultural Enginnccring, Silsoe, Occ. Paper No. 14

Morris, R.M. (1988) The synoptic-dynamical evolution of the storm of 15/16 October 1987, *Meteorological Magazine*, **117**, 293–306

Morton, J., Ogeden, J. and Hughes, T. (1984) *To Save a Forest: Whirinaki*, Bateman, Auckland, New Zealand

Mulgan, A. (1939) *The City of the Strait*, Whitcombe and Tombs, Wellington, New Zealand

Myers, N. (1980) *Conversion of Tropical Moist Forests*, National Academy of Sciences, Washington DC

New Zealand Official Year Book (1881–1961) Govt. Printer, Wellington, New Zealand

New Zealand Department of Conservation (1983) *New Zealand Forest Cover 1880 and 1980*, Govt. Printer, Wellington, New Zealand

Newcombe, K. (1984) *An Economic Justification for Rural Afforestation: The Case of Ethiopa*, World Bank, Energy Dept. Paper No. 16, Washington, D.C. p.16.

Nordstrom, K.F. and Allen, J.R. (1980) Geormorphologically compatible solutions to beach erosion, *Zeit für Geom., Supp. vol.* **34**, 142–154

Oakley, K.P. (1945) Some geological effects of a cloud burst in the Chilterns, *Records of Buckinghamshire*, **15**, 265–280

Oke, T.R. (1988) The urban energy balance, *Progress in Physical Geography*, **12**, 471–508

Palutikof, J. (1983) The impact of weather and climate on industrial production in Great Britain, *Journal of Climatology*, **3**, 65–79

Park, C.C. (1990) *Acid Rain: rhetoric and reality*, Routledge, London

Pearce, A.J. (1976) Magnitude and frequency of erosion by Hortonian overland flow, *J. Geology*, **84**, 65–80

Pielka, R.A. (1990) *The Hurricane*, Routledge, London

Poland, J.F. (ed.) (1984) *Guidebook to Studies of Land Subsidence Due to Groundwater Withdrawal*, UNESCO, Paris

Poland, J.F., Lofgren, D.B. and Pugh, R.G. (1975) *Land Subsidence in the San Joaquin Valley as of 1972*, US Geol. Surv. Prof. Paper, 437–H

Polunin, D. and Huxley, A. (1965) *Flowers of the Mediterranean*, Chatto & Windus, London

Prandini, L. *et al.* (1977) Behaviour of the vegetation in slope stability: a critical review, *Bull. Int. Assoc. Eng. Geol.*, **16**, 51–55

Pyne, S.J. (1982) *Fire in America*, Princeton University Press, Princeton, NJ

Rackham, O. (1980) *Ancient Woodland: its History, Vegetation and Uses in England*, Arnold, London

Rackham, O. (1986) *The History of the Countryside*, Dent, London

Rackham, O. (1989) *The Last Forest, the Story of Hatfield Forest*, Dent, London

Reed, A.H. (1979) Accelerated erosion of arable soils in the United Kingdom by rainfall and runoff, *Outlook on Agriculture*, **10**, 41–48

Reynolds, R. (1988) A chronical of the storm of 15th and 16th October, 1987, *NERC News*, **4**, 13–16.

Riley, D. and Young, A. (1966) *World Vegetation*, CUP, Cambridge

Robinson, D.A. and Boardman, J. (1988) Cultivation practice, sowing season and soil erosion on the South Downs, England: a preliminary study, *Journal Agricultural Science*, Cambridge, **110**, 169–177

Robinson, D. and Blackman, J. (1989) Soil erosion, soil conservation and agricultural policy for arable land in the UK, *Geoforum*, **20**, 83–92

Robinson, D. and Williams, R. (1988) Making waves in Downland Britain, *Geographical Mag.*, **60** (10), 40–45

Robinson, M., Clayton, M.C. and Henderson, W.C. (1990) The extent of field drainage in Scotland 1983–6, *Scottish Geographical Magazine*, **106**, 141–147

Rosenbaum, M.S. (1989) Geological influence on tunnelling under the Western Front at Vimy Ridge, *Proc. Geol. Assoc.*, **100**, 135–140

Roy, A. (1990) Countdown to the big one, *Geographical Mag.*, **62**, (12), 44–48

Rubey, W.W. (1952) *Geology and Mineral Resources of the Hardin and Brussel's Quadrangle, Illinois*, US Geol. Surv. Prof. Paper, 218

Ryan, C. (1985) Pests and problems: old man's beard, *Soil and Water*, **21**, 13–17

Saull, R.J. (1983) Soil erosion by water, problems and prospects; a study at the farm scale, Unpub. dissertation, Sheffield, University of Sheffield

Schumm, S.A. (1956) The role of creep and rainwash on the retreat of badlands slopes, *Am. J. Sci.*, **254**, 693–706

Searle, G. (1975) *Rush to Destruction*, A. H. and A.W. Reed, Wellington, New Zealand

Sedjo, R.A. and Clawson, M. (1984) Global forests, in Simon, J.L. and Kahn, H. (eds.) *Resourceful Earth*, Basil Blackwell, Oxford

Sharp, A. *et al.* (1982) Weathering of the balustrade on St Paul's Cathedral, London, *Earth Surface Processes and Landforms*, 7, 387–389.

Sherburne, R.W. (1988) Ground shaking and engineering studies on the Parkfield section of the San Andreas fault zone, *Earthquakes and Volcanoes*, **20**, 72–77

Sherlock, R.L. (1922) *Man as a Geological Agent*, Wetherby, London

Smith, C.J. (1980) *Ecology of the English Chalk*, Academic Press, London

Smith, K. and Tobin, G.A. (1979) *Human Adjustment to the Flood Hazard*, Longman, London

Smith, M. (1990) A tale of death and destruction, *Geographical Mag*, **62**, (3), 10–14

Stevens, G.R. (1974) *Rugged Landscape: The Geology of Central New Zealand*, A.H. and A.W. Reed, Wellington, New Zealand

Stevens, G. (1980) *New Zealand Adrift: The Theory of Continental Drift in a New Zealand Setting*, A. H. and A. W. Reed, Wellington, New Zealand

Stocking, M. (1976) Predicting erosion, *Geogr. Assoc. Rhodesia, Proceedings*, **9**, 27–36

Stoddart, D. (1963) Effects of hurricane Hattie on the British Honduras reefs and cays, October 30–31, 1961, *Atoll Research Bulletin*, **95**, 1–142

Sturroch, J.W. (1981) Shelter boosts crop yield by 35 per cent: also prevents lodging, *New Zealand Journal of Agriculture*, **143**, 18–19

Tabbush, P.M. and Williamson, D.R. (1987) *Rhododendron ponticum* as a forest weed, *Forestry Commission Bulletin*, **73**

Taylor, J. (1989) The British bracken problem, *Geography Review*, **2**, 7–11

Ternan, T.L. (1979–82) Soil erosion in the Lower Tamar Valley, south-west England, *Soils Discussion Group Proceedings*, 87–100

Thorarinsson, S. *et al.* (1973) The eruption of Heimaey, Iceland, *Nature*, **241**, 372–375

Thurgood, J.V. (1981) *Man and the Mediterranean Forest*, Academic Press, London

Tiwari, A.K., Mehta, J.S., Goel, O.P. and Singh, J.J. (1986) Geo-forestry of landslide affected areas in part of Central Himalaya, *Environmental Conservation*, **13**, 299–309

Tomlinson, G. (1983) Air pollution and forest decline, *Environmental Science and Technology*, **17**, 246–256

US Forest Service (1980) *An Assessment of the Forest and Rangeland Situation in the US*, US Department of Agriculture, Washington DC

Ulrich, B. (1983) Interaction of forest canopies with atmospheric constituents: SO_2, alkali and earth alkali cations and chloride, in Ulrich, B. and Pankrath, J. (eds.) *Effects of Accumulation of Air Pollutants in Forest Ecosystems*, Reidel, Dordrecht, The Netherlands, 33–45

UNFAO (United Nations Food and Agriculture Organisation) (1985) *Yearbook of Forest Products 1983*, FAO, Rome

United Nations (1977) *Desertification: Its Causes and Consequences*, UN Conference Proceedings, Nairobi

Walsh, M.J. (1981) Farm income production and exports: Part II, in Deane, R.S., Nicholl, P.W.E. and Walsh, M.J., *External Economic Structure and Policy, an Analysis of New Zealand's Balance of Payments*, Reserve Bank of New Zealand, Wellington

Ward, I. (1976) *New Zealand Atlas*, Govt Printer, Wellington, New Zealand

Warrick, R. and Farmer, G. (1990) The greenhouse effect, climatic change and rising sea level: implications for development, *Trans. Inst. Brit. Geographers*, NS **15**, 5–20.

WASCO (Water and Soil Conservation Authority) (1987) *The Whareama Story*, New Zealand Water and Conservation Authority, **64**, 1–20

Wheelwright, J. (1989) The rain forest myth, *Geographical Mag.*, **61** (4), 22–24

White, G. (1851) *The Natural History of Selbourne*, ed. E. Jesse, Bohn, London

World Bank (1984) Economic analysis issues in Bank financed forestry projects, World Bank AGR. Technical note, draft, 54

World Resources (1986) World Resources Inst. and International Inst. for Environment and Development, Basic Books, New York

Wright, L.W. (1980) Decision making and the logging industry: an example from New Zealand, *Biological Conservation*, **18**, 101–115.

WSDNZ (Water and Soil Division, New Zealand) (1969) *Land Use Capability Survey Handbook*, Water and Soil Division, Ministry of Works, Wellington, New Zealand

WWF (World Wildlife Fund) News (1987) Zimbabwe, *WWF News*, **45**, 3

Young, A. (1969) Present rate of land erosion, *Nature*, London, **224**, 851–852